Trouping in the

Oregon Country

TROUPING in the OREGON COUNTRY

A History of Frontier Theatre

by

ALICE HENSON ERNST

GREENWOOD PRESS, PUBLISHERS
WESTPORT, CONNECTICUT

Library of Congress Cataloging in Publication Data

Ernst, Alice Henson.
    Trouping in the Oregon country.

    Reprint of the ed. published by the Oregon
Historical Society, Portland.
    Bibliography: p.
    1. Theater--Northwest, Pacific--History.
I. Title.
[PN2273.N6E7 1974]   792'.09795   74-15552
ISBN 0-8371-7821-5

PN
2273
N6
E7
1974

Reprinted in 1974 by Greenwood Press,
a division of Williamhouse-Regency Inc.

Library of Congress Catalog Card Number 74-15552

ISBN 0-8371-7821-5

Printed in the United States of America

FOR THE PROMPTERS

ACKNOWLEDGMENTS

And who, then, are the 'prompters?'

. . . Off-stage figures, whose timely words have wakened thought, or given potent aid, in the making of this book.

From college days, Vernon Louis Parrington, needling a spellbound class with rapier questions: What, after all, has our youthful American culture achieved? How does the frontier fit in here? Where does all this movement take us? . . . Avid discussion of background material of his provocative *Main Currents in American Thought*.

Neighbor in time, a courtly figure with actor's face and voice, dissecting plays turned in by his "47 Workshop" at Fay House, Cambridge; the same fluent voice, probing visions of the Great American Play at Yale School of Drama: George Pierce Baker, of revered memory . . . Voices now stilled.

From the more urgent present, a rugged, Paul Bunyan voice, crying shame that the lively tale of Oregon's early theatres had never been set down, though to the south and north the doings of pioneer troupers had been given ample record: Stewart Holbrook, ex-thespian, whose foreword stands herein. Later sage advice has been soundly constructive.

In the gathering of material, a host of friendly folk whose memories of stirring times have lent life or color to their recreation. Their name is legion, and they themselves would be impatient of long listings. To all such timely prompters, warm thanks are herewith tendered.

Creators of the theatre which is its theme have been among these: George L. Baker, Northwest stage dynast who, not too long before his mortal exit, spoke with warmth and wisdom of the theatre's unique role; Louis "Butch" Fried, devoted backstage aide for practically every stage manager of the region from the glamorous New Market on. Edward Heilig contributed memories of his tycoon brother Calvin; Elizabeth Benedict, daughter of dynamic John P. Howe, reminisced as to his work in major Northwest theatres. Izetta Jewel, star of Baker Stock

Company days, renewed their famous charm during a recent visit. The keen memory and well-stocked mind of the late Henry Reed, first-hand observer of many of the events recorded, made a living narrative of vanished days.

Basic indeed has been a generous research grant from the University of Oregon, which made possible an extended study of available sources, either living or in early print. Grateful acknowledgment is here made to the graduate school, both for material aid and for leeway in shaping results. During repeat visits to key spots in a fading scene, the late Judge Fred Wilson of The Dalles, Mrs. Polly McKean Bell of Astoria, C. W. Brown of Canyon City, Murray Wade of Salem, Mrs. Gwynedde Maple of Empire, J. A. Matson of Marshfield, the late Myrtle P. Lee of Jacksonville, Mrs. Edward Kelly and Fletcher Fish of Medford, from a plethoric list, were generous of time and interest. From southern Oregon, Mrs. James (Edith Andrews) Stevens and her sister, Mrs. Grace Fiero, furnished documents and data as to their musical family. Miss Mertie Stevens and Mrs. William Hammond did likewise at Oregon City. At Portland, Mrs. Jack Methot, Mr. Sidney Zetosch and Charles von Rhein revived early theatre days. Doris Smith, Bess Whitcomb and Edris Morrison renewed its more recent stage.

The Washington scene received bright color from J. Willis Sayre, longtime drama critic for the Seattle *Times*. Glenn Hughes and John Conway, of the University School of Drama added friendly detail, as did Carl Landerholm of Vancouver.

During the evolution of the book, librarians throughout the entire region have contributed heavily to its bone and sinew of fact. Among them, Eleanor Stephens, former Oregon state librarian; Katherine Anderson of the Portland Public Library, Elizabeth Findly, reference librarian, University of Oregon, who made its index; Eva Santee of Vancouver and notably Priscilla Knuth of the Oregon Historical Society gave devoted aid. From without, George Freedley, curator of the Theatre Collection, New York Public Library, and the California Historical Society have furnished facts or photographs.

A series of illustrated theatre sketches written, at intervals of the study, for the Portland *Oregonian's* Sunday magazine called forth skilled cooperation from Sunday editors Jalmar Johnson and John Armstrong. Cordial appreciation is herewith recorded. Heartening also were numerous letters from interested readers during the spinning of an untold tale.

Credit for the unusual photo of theatre bills on page 112 is due to Dean Bond.

Colleagues on the Oregon campus have stood by valiantly, among them the late Randall Mills and his wife, Hazel E. Mills, and Martin Schmitt of the University Library's Special Collections.

The archives of the Oregon Historical Society library at Portland have for many years furnished a congenial base for intensive work. Warm thanks are due its able director and general editor Thomas Vaughan for constructive interest and for valued aid during publication of the manuscript, and to the state Society for the publication of this special study in its Western Imprints program.

Insistent prompters have been the players themselves—the gay and gallant troupers who did so much to make a bitter frontier a more gracious and worthwhile place to live. May these pages give back some fragment of their ageless valor!

A.H.E.

CONTENTS

ILLUSTRATIONS

INTRODUCTION

The United States and Great Britain were still disputing sovereignty when the first formal curtain, handsomely decorated with a painting of Mount Hood, went up in the Oregon Country. The play was a jolly farce. It was presented by the officers and men of H.B.M. Sloop of War *Modeste,* Captain Baillie, which mounted eighteen guns and was anchored in the Columbia River at Fort Vancouver, as indication that the flag followed the empire even to this remote post of the Hudson's Bay Company.

There had been increasing friction between the swarming American settlers and the British personnel of the fort, to say nothing of its trappers, during the joint occupancy of the vast region. It appears to have been the wise heads of the hoary old fur company who suggested that the mounting resentment and tension might be softened if Captain Baillie's young men staged a series of plays, dances, curling matches and such, to which the Americans should be invited. Thus the first formal curtain arose from motives not wholly concerned with box office, or even Theatre.

This is the event with which Alice Henson Ernst begins her account of more than a century of the theatre in Oregon. The seagoing actors of the *Modeste* may well have been very good, but they were amateurs, and professional troupers did not appear until the decade of the fifties, when magicians, phrenologists, readers, a circus or two, and what the author calls "a valiant handful of real play actors" started to assault Oregon City, the then metropolis of Oregon Territory, and to tour the newer settlements. They played wherever an audience waited, in court-houses, church parlors, hotel dining rooms, saloons, and under canvas.

Fortunately for the record, the press had arrived on the scene ahead of the troupers. The *Spectator* was established just in time to greet the *Modeste's* company, and other newspapers soon fol-lowed, their editors ready to comment, either lyrically or acidly, according to their nature and digestions, on the fare provided by the wandering minstrels and thespians. Indeed, the new *Oregonian* of new Portland displayed the classic frontier at its unpredictable best by publishing serially a home-grown play by W. H. Adams, a covered wagon pioneer, which is believed to be the first book of an original nature produced in the Northwest. Done in galloping blank verse, it was a hard-hitting political satire with "the sting of a scorpion."

It is one of Mrs. Ernst's many merits that she keeps the reader aware of the swiftly changing scene, as the vague and doubtful Oregon Country became two immense territories, then was made into whole or parts of five states of the Union. She is careful meanwhile to mark the original settlements west of the Cascade Range and the so-called sagebrush country of eastern Oregon. Long before the railroads came, wagon shows were penetrating the latter region, where the intervals of civilization were separated by days rather than hours of travel; where the sun rose up straight out of level ground and sank back into the flat earth, and the lonely distances seemed somehow ominous to people accustomed to towns, or at least to hills. Many a mummer must have had the uneasy feeling he had been tricked into touring an enormous emptiness of sun and wind and mirage.

Sternwheelers meanwhile moved actors upon and down the Columbia and the Willamette, bringing entertainment to the misty landings, the rising sawmill towns, the salmon packing stations; and at last, when railroads connected Portland with St. Paul and San Francisco, there began a period of theatre comparable to that of longer settled and more populous parts of the West. Properly enough, Mrs. Ernst uses the splendid New Market Theatre on Portland's waterfront to typify this era of red plush and progress.

Here was elegance worthy the great names of the American and English theatres who played it, and worthy, too, the pride of Oregonians who had come in the days when the city of Portland whitewashed its many big stumps to render them less dangerous to night traffic, and when night music consisted, as a pioneer recalled, of the melancholy cadences of owls in the surrounding timber.

Opera houses were rising in Salem, in Albany, Eugene, Astoria, and The Dalles. They were piped for gas in chandeliers and footlights, while hanging from the flies or stacked in the wings were the diamond-dye scenery and the reversible sets with which a competent road company could stage almost anything from *Blue Jeans* to The Bard.

Elegance succeeded elegance, and the mauve decade of the nineties saw The Road approaching zenith. Stock companies filled their own houses, year in and out, or toured the lesser towns with a repertoire fit for a run of six nights and two matinees. The oldtime music halls became vaudeville theatres in chains booked from Chicago. The Chautauqua circuit hired William Jennings Bryan and all the bell ringers in Switzerland to fill the great brown tents with genteel folk who wanted Culture in homeopathic doses; but liked it even better when Buffalo Bill's Wild West came to town, and they saw the buckskinned god who sat his white horse so nonchalantly and shot the pretty balls into showers of tinkling glass, while a forty-two-piece band beat the daylights out of "The Stars and Stripes Forever."

They are all here in Mrs. Ernst's account. So is the exotic world of the Chinese theatre, and the half-world of the out-and-out honkytonks, and even the gypsy world of the rattlesnake oil and Kickapoo Indian Sagwa medicine shows. They are all here, for the writer rightly includes them as parts of the universal theatre. One and all, they began to fade at almost the same time the new art form of animated shadows moved out from the nickelodeon stories into Babylonish palaces where the shadows soon started to talk, after a fashion, and one could sit in darkness, eating popcorn and crackerjack, without a thought, in this new world of show business where all is black and white, even when it is done in Technicolor.

The Road was finished. So were stock and repertoire and vaudeville and circus and Chautauqua. As for the med shows, they were to survive in the form and style of radio announcers and comedians, merely waiting to put on the clean white coats and to pick up the stethoscopes required of TV doctors . . .

The need for the present book has been compounded by the virtual disappearance of the theatre not only in Oregon but elsewhere save, of course, in New York City. This is the first historical account of the stage in our region. Because it is as readable as it is thorough and comprehensive, it is also an important contribution to the stage in America. Mrs. Ernst has done us proud.

STEWART HOLBROOK

Portland, Oregon
December, 1960

Earliest extant Oregon Country playbill known.
(Courtesy Mrs. Belle Gillogly.)

FIRST AUDIENCE / *in a Last Frontier*

When the great migration westward began its outward push, it was toward a fabulous horizon. Geography gave it rough outline, to be sure, but mainly its boundaries were superlatives: the widest ocean at its far door; the steepest mountains at its back; the deepest fiords slashing its misty coast; the stillest, greenest forests at its heart. The tall tale had come in with the explorer's coon-skin cap, and had stayed there, happily at home in the tall timber on the Pacific.

Something about its vast backdrop nudged the timid mind; its actors were strictly new-world: that huge man named Paul, with his giant Blue Ox, casually scooping out Puget Sound; its voyageurs and trappers singing along lost rivers; its lumberjacks with their sizzling oaths; a noble savage or two strategically placed. It was all incredibly fresh and provocative to a nation just then leaning on its creative hoe, and on a gargantuan scale to set the blood pounding. Grapevine rumors from the Oregon Country told of timber pricking the sky; of lush soil needing only to be tickled; of donation claims crying out for takers—though, by the same token, of bob cats hefty as mountain lions. No wonder the worn New Englander, coaxing niggard acres, the Southerner harried by the boll weevil, even the more prosaic plainsman took off post haste for a modern Eden, leaving plows and mules untended. Some good hard-fisted Adams and Eves were needed, obviously. And let the serpent beware.

It was no wonder, in the footloose forties, that the stage folk got under way early. They loved adventure, they adored new audiences. Going West, those restless days, was far more than a slogan: it was a state of mind. Tucking a hasty script or two into capacious carpet bags, the troupers arrived soon after the exhausted settlers. They found it native land. But even before the stage folk climbed up on make-shift platforms, curtains had been rising in the new frontier, often without benefit of footlights. Folk entertainment—eager, spontaneous—does not always await the proscenium arch.

In any region, the amusements of its early settlers fall into broad and lively patterns, deeply etched by human need. The stomp of dancing feet on puncheon floors, the fiddle's exultant song, release the same emotions in Kentucky or Connecticut. The folk tale, told in Yankee twang, in southern drawl or in the flatter vowels of the plainsman, have in common the goings-on of villains or heroes known from Maine to Arizona, though, like the four-footed creatures which bear them company, they take on local color here or there. The nostalgic ballad, precursor of our modern blues, travelling outward by swift underground, retains strong family likenesses wherever found. Frankie and Johnny refuse to be penned up within state lines. And how readily they lock elbows with Lili Marlene overseas!

In the Oregon Country as elsewhere before the players, entertainment was mainly impromptu. Music played a large part—thrummed along a tedious trail, fiddled on puncheon floors, or hymned out in crude log cabin meeting houses. Everybody took part, and everybody meant settler, drifter, housewife, doxy. Few props were needed: given a lively banjo or two and some lusty voices, you had the makings of a rousing evening. Dancing, spontaneous as speech, was fully as universal. Wall raisings, quilting or husking bees and such functional affairs drew hearty crowds; charades and aspiring amateur skits or readings enlivened weary evenings. They lifted the spirits of settlers engaged in hand-to-hand conflict with the soil. But all such transient events are largely unrecorded; the newspapers were later in coming; yellowed hand-written diaries give only scattered mention. Since boundaries are urgent in so vast a domain, let us at once invoke the useful curtain—symbol of the arranged or rehearsed program, and with the troupers mount their rough-hewn stages.

The first recorded curtain in the Oregon Country is suitably dramatic, the occasion of its presentation deeply rooted in the region's growth.

* * *

Off-stage, the drums of war were rolling in the new frontier, in the raw forties of its active settlement. Tension was high between England and America, knotted about prior rights of domain, from explorations or loose treaty. In the bold footsteps of Lewis and

Clark and the later trail of Astor's overlanders, eager Americans pressed in upon a wilderness reserved by British fur companies for operation of their roving brigades. Only the trapper, the lonely *coureur du bois,* protected by royal grant, ranged the forest and marsh for rich peltries later to be sold in China, in Russia, in the world's sleekest capitals. A few lank mountain men in search of beaver threaded the hidden streams. It was in the interest of the fur companies to hold the wilderness in its primal state; the new-comers as clearly needed the mile square of land promised by the American government to all homeseekers for their living needs. Clashes between settlers and roving employees of the far-flung Hudson's Bay Company increased sharply. At last, to safeguard the interests of their London firm and to head off possible open conflict, a modest emissary was dispatched. Its place in Northwest annals is far too little known.

Dropping anchor well off-shore from Fort Vancouver, far western trade headquarters of the Bay Company, there appeared on October 11, 1845, H.B.M.S. *Modeste,* Capt. Thomas Baillie—one of a "fleet of war vessels visiting the North Pacific ocean." Friendly in spite of her eighteen guns, manned by officers notable for the amenities and a lively crew, the sloop of war proceeded to make history in her own way.

Cut off from the pleasures and excitements of civilization, its personnel faced the wilderness with good humor and wisdom. Friendly relations with the scattered settlers farming the rich bottom lands along the Columbia River were soon established; tools and food exchanged as well as social courtesies. There were dancing parties, on shore and off. At last, "in return for the hospitality of settlers," the *Modeste* announced performance of a group of plays, to be staged by her enlisted men and officers, with feminine roles played by the settlers' daughters. Duly, on February 3, 1846, arose the first recorded curtain in the Oregon Country.

The plays selected were gay and cosmopolitan in mood: two short comedies, *The Mayor of Garrett* and *Three Weeks of Marriage,* with a concluding farce, *The Deuce is in Him.* The curtain, painted by the sailor-actors, represented nearby Mount Hood. The pleased audience warmly applauded a brief prologue by a cast member which ended: *"Modeste is our ship, and modest are we."* News of the exciting event spread throughout the region—a far cry indeed, since the Oregon Country then embraced the present states of Oregon, Washington and Idaho, with portions of Wyoming and Montana.

The press—a struggling semi-monthly newspaper published at Oregon City, capital of the provisional government—was lyric in praise. The *Oregon Spectator,* first paper to be published west of the Mississippi, in its second issue, February 19, 1846, included a section on "Theatrical Entertainment." An unknown critic noted that "A sailor's life is full of excitement," and continued: "the happy crew" of the *Modeste,* to escape monotony, have "formed a little theatrical company among themselves (the first, by the way in Oregon)" . . . in their plays "sustaining the characters in the most creditable manner, that even had Will Shakespeare himself looked up, he could not say nay." Shakespeare's opinion is of course moot, but existing comment on this first performance leaves no doubt that the play-starved pioneers were delighted.

Praise for the settlers' daughters was by no means lacking, among fervid details of portrayals of masculine roles. As for the hosts, "the scenery painted by themselves is really beautiful." The orchestra, too, was "well got up, with violin, flute and the harmonious bagpipe" — an unusual musical combination, but undoubtedly stirring. "We conclude," continues the rapt critic, "by saying that we wish these supporters of the drama every prosperity and success, and bid them God Speed. Gratified, I think we may say in my own name and that of other settlers in Oregon shall we be when we see the curtain raised in our infant city, and entertainments offered us equal to that of the 'modest' bluejackets." With characteristic verve, the stage annals of the Oregon Country were under way.

It is interesting to note that the theatre arrived in California by a comparable route, though at a somewhat later date. It is recorded, by Constance Rourke in her *Troupers of the Gold Coast,* that "At Monterey, in the spring of 1848, the wing of a long adobe house was fitted up (for the soldiers of Stevenson's regiment) as a theatre . . . Here they produced stout old English farces and even Shakespeare . . . At Sonoma in the Valley of the Moon another company of the regiment turned to theatricals at about the same time, and played for four months in a miniature theatre." San Francisco also witnessed plays in the spring of 1848, given by "a few stragglers of fortune"—these, aside from some local Spanish fiestas, being the first recorded dramatic performances in the southern territory.

The somewhat earlier performance at Fort Vancouver (February 3, 1846) was followed by others during the same winter and spring; indeed it is implied that tryout programs may have preceded the one made permanent by the *Spectator*. The Corps Dramatique meanwhile shared actively in the everyday life about them. "Captain Baillie and the gunroom officers of the *Modeste*," we learn, "entertained a numerous circle at a ball," attended by a "brilliant assemblage of the fair sex of Oregon . . . Reels, country dances, figures of eight and jigs being the order of the evening." Three of the *Modeste's* officers also attended the Washington's Birthday Ball at Oregon City, their gentlemanly behavior, "uniting olio cum dignitate," drawing editorial praise.

A repeat performance on May 14, 1846, added the "musical and favorite comedies" *Love in a Village* and *The Mock Doctor* to *The Mayor of Garrett* earlier given. Included also was a picnic on the "dairy plains" fringing the fort, sponsored by Captain Baillie. To this second fete guests from all over the Oregon Country were bidden, settlers and prominent persons from as far off as the "Tuality Plains," the Willamette Valley, and Portland, then but a straggling river hamlet. Years later, one reminiscent guest, staunch Isaac Newell, master of the barge *Great Mogul,* plying out from Canemah, near Oregon City, relayed a vivid eye-witness account of these first plays in the *West Shore,* May 1879, sharing—thirty years later—another dramatic high moment: a performance of *The Lady of Lyons* at Portland's splendid New Market Theatre, soaring three stories high and fully gaslighted. The contrast between the two scenes, amusingly told in the words of an ancient mariner, is striking indeed.

Nothing could have been more arresting than the backdrop of the Northwest's first curtain: the fort's looming palisades, etched darkly against a somber forest; the bold contours of a sloop of war; the gay uniforms of the *Modeste's* officers; the homespuns of the settlers; the feminine finery of their women. Dominating it all, a giant figure, the "White-Headed Eagle"—John McLoughlin, chief factor of the Hudson's Bay Company, later McLoughlin of Oregon by wry adoption. There was drama everywhere: in the triumphant return of homing fur brigades, bateaux awash with cargo, oars high in salute, exultant in song as they rounded the Point to their beloved Belle Plaine; in the brooding silence of hovering Indians, resentful of the white man's invasion of their ancient heritage. But mainly in the sheer boldness of this human handful, flung against the wilderness in an attempt to carve an empire.

Some slight gift of grace must have been added to the raw frontier by the aspiring thespians. "Vancouver has during the week presented a display of beauty, fashion and Gaity [*sic*]," writes someone in the *Spectator* signing himself "A Plain Man." "The Modeste's entertainments . . . have made our locality quite a scene of animation." The winter of '47 saw more plays: *High Life Below Stairs, The Irish Widow,* plus the conventional farce. The settlers' daughters won special mention for "improved good taste in costumes;" continued success for the popular programs was warmly bespoken.

But, unknown to the actors, the flaming issue of national boundaries with its shrill battle cry, "Fifty-Four Forty or Fight," had by now been settled far off-stage, and by compromise. Though concluded on June 15, 1846, this vital fact did not reach the distant frontier until the following November, when the bark *Toulon* dropped anchor from the Sandwich (Hawaiian) Islands, then closely bound by trade with the Oregon Country. The gay plays of this second season thus took on the nature of a farewell. Under the heading, "FORTHCOMING DEPARTURE OF THE MODESTE," the *Spectator* pays tribute to her captain and crew who, in leaving the territory, "Carry with them assurances of high esteem from a host of acquaintances." Genuine regret was registered when she finally lifted anchor on May 31, 1847. Long after, the White-Headed Eagle, then retired, could write: "I am convinced that it was owing to the Modeste being at Vancouver, and the gentlemanly conduct of Capt. Baillie and his officers and the good discipline of the crew that the officials of Hudson's Bay

Company had less trouble." In a tense international moment, the drama had played its part well.

By the treaty of partition of 1846, Fort Vancouver was left on American soil, along with the vast stretch of Oregon Country up to the forty-ninth parallel, our present boundary. But the mood set by its first curtain lingered. The fort, center of northwestern trade, supplying the Sandwich Islands, California, the Russian settlements of far Alaska, was also its social center—and unexpectedly brilliant. As head of the powerful Hudson's Bay Company, McLoughlin lived in baronial style. Surrounded by retainers, with bagpipes skirling, dinners were served on Wedgewood, Spode or Chinese Willow; candles gave back the gleam of crystal or silver from buckskin garments. The good doctor himself esteemed old-world manners. With impressive ceremony, visitors were piped ashore, and these were many and distinguished—world travellers, writers, missionaries, men of science. They could linger at will in this wilderness oasis, at times dubbed the "New York of the Pacific Coast." Thomas Nuttall, John K. Townsend and David Douglas, the artist Paul Kane, the Whitmans, were warmly welcomed. Here too settlers exchanged produce for scarce seed or cattle. "McLoughlin's kind treatment of these newcomers," it has been stated, "helped to foster the growth of an American settlement of the region, a population which was to an appreciable extent responsible for winning the area and the 49th parallel for the United States."* The good-humored blessing of the jolly tars had followed through.

Surface change occurred with the later transfer of the Bay Company's main depot to Fort Victoria. A new flag whipped the breeze; the uniforms changed color. But life at Vancouver, "the garrison," as it was now called, retained its gracious charm. Travel was easier; plays flourished with even greater vigor. Staged now by American officers and their men, results were fully as lively—and as literate. The officers read Shakespeare with their men; all loved to spout melodrama, to put on minstrel shows or blackface skits; backstage work was a welcome change from barracks monotony. In 1853, while a young lieutenant named Ulysses S.

*Quoted in H. H. Bancroft, *History of Oregon* (San Francisco, 1886-88), 1:576, footnote 6, citing McLoughlin's private papers.

Grant was briefly in residence, the Garrison Players put on at the Officers' Club at Fort Vancouver a play highly favored at the time, *The Golden Farmer* by Benjamin Webster. Eked out by the usual farce and various romantic ballads, it was greatly enjoyed by nearby civilians. It was all agreeably versatile, and until far down in the '80s, acting groups from the garrison, under changing names, flung down their challenge to the vast distances and threatening loneliness of the Oregon Country. Balls and fetes still drew the "Oregon fair" from nearby donation farms along the Columbia (Vancouver itself not yet a town); from gangling Portland, swiftly outgrowing its river banks; from the rich farmlands of the Willamette Valley.

In most of the ragged hamlets of the Oregon Country, however, life was by no means so gay an affair. Oregon City, south on the Willamette, was a hive of activity. Here, a clot of settlers had congealed around a rough sawmill begun by McLoughlin at a sharp fall of the river; incoming Americans had added stores and a crude woolen mill. Briefly capital of the provisional government, and from 1849 to 1851 territorial capital, here the politicos were gathering. But so too were the players.

And a motley lot they were: magicians, phrenologists, readers, circuses, among a valiant handful of real play actors. The magicians led off first. Earliest noted, in the scant array of professionals for the fifties, was a group of travelling magicians, the Messrs. Hubbell and Rossiters' "Great Exhibition (Legerdemain)," from California. "Well spoken of," they performed at Oregon City on August 29, 1851, and were billed to tour the upper country later, exhibiting in the larger villages. Pushed by necessity, the amateurs were brave in these lean years, some of them achieving near-professional status. One such group were members of Professor Newell's music class in Oregon City. So successful was their costumed cantata, "Flora's Festival," staged at the courthouse in 1854, that it won repeat performances in nearby towns: at Portland, in August of the same year, at Salem, the year following. Even the distant San Francisco press gave it notice.

Yes, life was difficult those days. Though the cantata achieved the crowning honor: performance at the Fourth of July celebration of its home town, for "the thousand lovers of good music who are

y

8/

expected to throng our city for that occasion," a partial repetition that same year (1855) had to be "indefinitely postponed . . . on account of the present excitement growing out of the Indian wars . . ." The drums of war, never long silent, were beating out concerted Indian attacks throughout the Pacific Northwest: at Crescent City on the south coast; along the Rogue and Umpqua rivers; northward to Tillamook; in eastern Oregon, a stubborn blaze at Powder River. Far to the north, Washington saw its later climax at Fort Steilacoom, with the killing of Colonel Slaughter and three of his men . . .

But if life was rugged in the tall tree country, so too were the troupers. They played wherever an audience waited: in court-houses, in hotel dining rooms, in church parlors, and—if need be, in friendly taverns. Up in the high Sierras, the roving Chapman family used the sawed-off stump of a giant redwood as stage . . . It was the play that mattered, not the place.

And, everywhere along the way, certain trailblazers emerge. Playing at Oregon City for three nights in December of 1856 "with deserved success before going on to Portland" was the Thoman Theatrical Company, billed the next year in other Willamette Valley hamlets. Other professionals widely listed, mainly from the south, are the Graves Family in concerts, "with singing and dancing by Miss Louise." Breathtaking in scope is a program billed at Washington Hall in Oregon City for December, 1857. In this, "Professor" Vandorff promised "A Panoramic Entertainment including a Scientific Lecture dealing with the Planetary System," a panorama of the Bible, together with "Spiritual Manifestations . . . and Exhibitions of Mesmerism and Ventriloquism." The long-haired 'professors' were very much on stage those days, offering practically everything from phrenology to readings of the classics.

Less esoteric, but probably more satisfying was the appearance of noted character actor Dan Gates, famed along the entire West Coast for his impersonations of distinguished orators and actors, who drew crowded houses in Oregon City the following November.

The unpredictable frontier has its own surprises—dramatic and otherwise. Somewhat unexpectedly, the first book "of an original nature published in the Oregon country" was a play.

Written by the editor of the *Oregon Argus*, W. L. Adams, who had come west by covered wagon, it was a hard-hitting political satire called *Treason, Stratagems and Spoils*, by "Breakspear." Done in galloping blank verse (1852), it first ran in serial form in the new-born Portland *Oregonian*. So effectively did it lampoon certain well-known political figures (Democrats) that it became an immediate best seller, sending settlers scurrying to the general store. Crude but powerful woodcuts enlivened its pages. Its rough-hewn humor still bears a scorpion sting.

At Oregon City in 1856 there now alighted briefly a trouper extraordinary, a Marco Polo among players. This was Stephen Massett, in whose pungent memoirs, *Drifting About, or What Jeems Pipes Saw and Did*, the raw frontier was to receive highly candid, and at times acid treatment. In his eccentric Paul Bunyan strides, we may retrace something of the uncomfortable adventures of his footloose brotherhood.

Massett, an actor of some attainments, on leaving his native England for the New World, briefly supported several stalwarts of the New York stage. Swift prey to the current gold fever, he gave to San Francisco its "first real dramatic performance" in the old courthouse in Portsmouth Square. His lively one-man show featured numerous ballads, some written by himself, scattered among clever impersonations. Climax of the program was his famous "Yankee Town Meeting," in which he gave "mutations" of seven different persons assembled for the purpose of "suppressing the press"—a razor strop vendor, a baritone opera singer and such bizarre types. Aided only by a piano—one of three or four to be found in the West—the black-mustachioed singer with the grand manner was highly successful. Tickets were three dollars each, and front seats were reserved for ladies.

Not even a profit of $500 or the throbbing life of San Francisco could long stay his gypsy foot. Journeys to the Sandwich Islands, to Italy, to France, eased the itch somewhat, followed by tours of the California gold mines. Then, deciding to see something of the fabled Oregon Country before going 'down under' to Australia, he embarked by the steamer *Columbia* for Crescent City, first port of entry in the new frontier. There the trailing wet queues of Chinese coolies unloading freight in the surf — there were no wharves — engaged his roving eye. Blithely fronting the unknown, he steamed farther north, pausing at those few towns large enough to provide audiences. Among these were Portland and Astoria, of which we shall speak later.

His visit to Oregon City, in August of 1856, was mainly to buy a horse, on which he was to venture some 300 miles into the wilds. He had arrived by flatboat: because of low water the steamer *Jennie Clark* could not reach the city. The town he found "deadly lively," though he himself records some agreeable acquaintances, and the local press an appreciative audience. With his melodeon, a pint-sized organ favored by performers of the day, strapped to a mule, he proceeded on his way. We shall later catch up with this redoubtable trouper in his invasion of rural Oregon.

Throughout the Oregon Country, the circuses trod hard on the more sedate heels of magicians and phrenologists. They were even more fully enjoyed; so much so that they need their own special place. Here we need only note that Oregon City, during the fifties, turned out briskly for the Mammoth Circus, earlier "visited by more than 70,000 during the tour of California mining towns, Sacramento and San Francisco." Daring equestrian slack rope performers, jugglers and equilibrists, the Clown of Clowns with his "educated dogs" claimed rapt attention. Other Willamette Valley stops before doubling south again were Salem, Silverton, French Prairie, Champoeg, and Portland. The Olympic Circus, with band, also struck tents there in October of the next year (1858), advertising artists from the pioneer Rowe's Circus, known up and down the coast. Lee's National Circus and Roman Amphitheatre performed in July of '59, "decidedly the most complete in the United States," with gymnasts, rope performers, trained ponies, "before a circle of admiring supporters."

The love of the settlers for such earthy exhibitions was sharply reproved by Editor Adams of the *Argus,* commending to his townspeople a lecture on astronomy, illustrated by lantern slides, by a Mr. Carter, billed in December, 1857. Remarking that since "our citizens are generally liberal in patronizing monkey shows and travelling oddities," he "doubts not they will exhibit commendable zeal for a scientific exhibition."

Yet all was not raw spectacle in this last frontier. Oregon City, site of McLoughlin's operations as far back as 1829, was the first incorporated town west of the Rocky Mountains in 1844. It is hard to remember that in the latter year such future urban giants as Chicago or San Francisco were fellow hamlets. By the fifties Oregon City had churches, streets, lodges, woolen and flouring mills, the first hotel and newspaper in the region, and an aspiring culture. A cosmopolitan note intrudes with notice of Shakespearean readings by the French actress, Mlle. Duret, "well known throughout Europe." From headquarters in Portland she gave at Oregon City "one of her grand drawingroom entertainments to an unusually crowded house." This urban tinge deepened soon after when Mr. and Mrs. Connor from California presented their "Original and Dramatic Entertainment," after reputed production in London and other world capitals. This featured a play written by Mrs. Connor, with a Kentucky hills background. With but two members in its cast, the local press found all parts of the play "perfect in every way." Some slight flaws might have been probed by a more detached view, but it seems evident that from the start the drama had devoted followers in the territory's first capital.

Down in southern Oregon, by contrast, a gold rush was in progress. Almost overnight, with the finding of placer gold at Rich's Gulch in January 1853, Jacksonville, one of the most exciting towns of the Oregon Country, sprang into roaring life—a drift of white tents on the astonished hills. Within weeks, every foot of the gulch was staked out and claimed. Later strikes on nearby tributaries of the Rogue River panned out oversized nuggets; discoveries of quartz in nearby hills fanned the excitement. During the late fifties, Jacksonville, oldest town in southern Oregon and center of the Rogue River gold rush, was for a time the largest and richest town in the state. Pay dirt from Jackson County alone ran up to $1,500,000 during its active years.

Straddling the Wells, Fargo stage route winding up through the high Sierras, the new northern camp attracted the usual ragtag of miners, tinhorn gamblers, floozies, traders: the assorted drift of shady characters drawn by the magnet of easy money. A steadier backbone of frontiersmen was there as well. Here was founded the first bank in the Oregon Country, and one of the first churches beyond the Mississippi (by good aid of the town's gamblers). The Sisters of Charity early added their calm strength to the scene. A trading post sprang up. Its wares, packed in by muleback from Crescent City, 120 miles distant on the coast, drew avid buyers from the nearby creeks. By day its narrow streets hummed with Mexican packers, red-shirted miners, long-queued Chinamen, silent Indians. By night the faro and monte games were in full swing.

Stage annals are scarce here in the fifties—life itself perhaps too much the stuff of drama. The Pacific Circus paused, swinging back to California from its northern arc at Portland; some unnamed strolling troupers playing at wayside inns or courthouses along the way; a local concert or two in an upstairs hall. An 1855 account from a diary in a nearby settlement describes an "Exhibition" at "Mr. Oatman's tavern" where the Drummond light was used to illuminate the scene. The program included a variety of scenes, from panoramas in Europe to the renowned *Pike County Traveller* and sleight of hand performances.

The taverns were friendly places those days. Jacksonville's Last Chance or its famed El Dorado gave warm refuge—albeit lively at times—to stage driver, miner, or if need be, to the roving player. For more sedate events, the settlers gathered in upstairs McCully's Hall.

At Ashland, twelve miles south—and a bare eighteen miles from the California border—the tale was much the same. Clustered around its grist mill, built in 1854, it had no sizable hall. For the rare dramatic events settlers drove the dozen miles to J'ville, as it was called. But when the Rogue gold rush was at its height, at a nearby camp on Althouse Creek an exotic visitor paused briefly. From Browntown, where a fabulous slug of pure gold had been found ($15,000), drift back reports of an appearance there by Lotta Crabtree, famed child actress later to become a favorite comedienne of the American stage. Trouping out from San Francisco with her shrewd Scotch mother at the tender age of nine, Lotta, as the stage remembers her, was showered with nuggets and pokes of gold dust thrown on stage by cheering miners. Grown up, she was to see more of the Northwest.

From the southern gold fields, stage and trade routes led northward to Scottsburg (Fort Scott) on the Umpqua River, or into the fertile Willamette Valley, by paths familiar to the troupers as well. And here, in these rural wilds, we shall rejoin black-mustachioed Stephen Massett, though he had approached them from the north. Steaming north from Crescent City, his main objective had been Astoria, "made classic by the immortal pen of Washington Irving," one of his favorite authors. There he planned to indulge a long-cherished whim: to declaim Bryant's "Thanatopsis" on the very spot "where rolls the Oregon, and hears no sound save his own dashings." And this he did, in an entertainment in the "flourishing little town." Impressed by its setting and marine possibilities, he predicted a glowing future as a world port.

On up the wide Columbia he sailed. "One of the most beautiful [rivers] I have ever seen. I have written from the Bosphorus, the Rhine, the Rhone, and the old Hudson," the actor muses, "yet I must proclaim from this distant region, the majesty, greatness, sublimity of this the finest of them all." He was en route for "Vancouver's, Depot for the U.S. Troops for the Territories of Oregon and Washington; and the 9th Infantry are at present stationed there . . . The officers of this garrison are noted for their attentions and hospitalities to strangers." The steamer presently stopped only to discharge freight at the "splendid storehouse and wharf," but on its return trip, on leaving Oregon, Massett there gave a concert "At Co. G's headquarters." Massett was royally received, leaving high praise for the American officers and their courtesy, and carrying an impression of the Hudson's Bay Company's "immense warehouses, filled with all sorts of merchandise from a toothpick to a bale of cotton." His initial concert at nearby Portland deserves somewhat more space.

Sharply contrasting with this brief urban interlude are the player's reaction toward Oregon's rural reaches. Duly equipped at Oregon City with a horse, a mule, and his faithful melodeon—described by Massett as "a cross between an accordion and a barrel organ"—the actor set forth for Salem, forty miles to the south. Charming scenery, he granted, but the food at roadside inns along the way brought forth the fervent comment: "primitive, and very peculiar." Mainly apples, greasy pork, bread dipped in molasses, "and some good water," even at a moderate six-bit rate it earned the verdict "cheap and nasty." At some of those so-called inns, too, the table manners of patrons greatly disturbed him: "jack-knives were far too much in evidence as tools; forks for toothpicks. "Hotel life in this country," he concludes "is perfectly awful."

Massett was not the only traveller to complain of the frontier's six-bit hotels—probably justly. But other contemporary accounts also enlarge on the neatness and hospitality of the Willamette Valley farms, with their white-painted houses and red barns—a New England heritage already strongly present. Most of them treasured heirlooms—a polished highboy, a silver teapot, a sampler which had survived the plains crossing.

Massett suffered many ills on this trip. Out from Oregon City, at a jolty turn, his melodeon was suddenly launched into a field by the balky mule. He lost his way continually. But, arrived at Salem, official capital of the territory since 1851, he presented his "Yankee Town Meeting," plus ballads, to a sizable audience gathered at the courthouse. The room was bravely lighted, in good frontier fashion, by candles—six tall ones. An unfeeling gust of wind chose the moment of his soulful rendering of "the Light of Other Days" to "blow 'em out." The audience roared with laughter. The minstrel's sense of humor somehow failed: he confides that "he didn't think much of it." But, with true aplomb, the show went on. So, later, did the trouper.

He next achieved up-valley Albany, which at that early day, by Massett's count, could muster only "75 souls"—slim pickings for a strolling minstrel. And though the citizen he approached — a blacksmith—obligingly ventured that he might "scare up ten or twelve," the artist declined the challenge. At nearby Corvallis he did risk a stop. Again, hospitality was profuse. Massett's memoirs reflect his intense surprise at protracted handshaking by his audience, who came up as a man vigorously to express appreciation of his efforts. This, too, with "the house quite full: so was the moon." Here, "a little scared about the Indians," and also by now somewhat troubled by difficulties as to his daily cold bath, the urban gentleman turned his steps northward.

On the return journey the artist was hospitably entertained at Salem "at the pleasant ranch house of some one formerly of Washington, D. C."; pleasant memories also of Oregon City. And so back to Portland.

Here, Massett at a lengthy steamer stop had earlier given "his first concert in Oregon." Portland, favorably located near river and sea, was already taking on urban airs. His appearance there, reports the *Oregonian* of August 2, 1856, called forth "the largest and most fashionable audience yet seen in the territory, which filled to overflowing the new hall of Keith's Metropolis Hotel. The ladies were out in great numbers, and the various entertainment . . . listened to with great attention." His comic portrayals, his rendition of such ballads as "The Old Arm Chair," his readings from *The Lady of Lyons,* and in particular his *tour de force,* "Thanatopsis," "made quite a sensation . . . which assured the artist of a warm reception on his return from Oregon City and Salem." But not so. This genial climate was definitely chilled, on the actor's return, by his faulty memory as to certain out-of-pocket loans. The sparse audiences of the valley tour had been a cruel blow. Far too familiar to the troupers was that horrid ailment: flat purse. Heading out for "parts unknown," he was later housemate for young Edwin Booth.

Even at Portland, dramatic events had been rare: some scattered exhibitions put on by the Portland Female Seminary (1855); a visit by Pacific Circus and Hippodrome — these latter "design travelling through the upper country, and will extend their tour to Jacksonville and the northern California mines." Not long after Massett's memorable visit, the cantata "Flora's Festival" was given by the "young zephyrs" from Oregon City. For this the Methodist church opened its doors.

In those ragged days, the Theatre meant upstairs halls, rough platform stages, largely bare of wings or scenery. Some ten years later Seattle's earliest dramatic events took place in the cookhouse of Yesler's sawmill. At older Olympia, wandering performers had found refuge, in the fifties, in a hotel dining room. California's high Sierra minning camps were a constant challenge to the players: blankets were often commandeered to shut off noisy bars; cotton window drapes might serve as backdrops. It was a battle of wits and sinew.

Down on Portland's riverfront, the town's first professional visitors paused for a rare holiday treat. "A Theatrical Corps has been in the city a few days, giving entertainment at National Hall on Front Street, to full and RESPECTABLE audiences," we read on December 27, 1856. "At the principal places in the Valley they have been received with crowded houses." This was the pioneer Thoman Theatrical Troupe, earlier billed at Oregon City, which the next year toured the entire territory. Professor Risley's "Red, White and Blue Varieties" soon followed. Mrs. Emily Lesdernier thrilled audiences with her "inimitable readings" of Shakespeare, visiting Corvallis, Salem and Oregon City as well. Professor Vandorff repeated at Portland his astounding mesmeric melange, and in the late fall, the Mammoth Circus put on one of its "Popular and Chaste" performances out on the fringe of town.

Notable stage figures soon appear: skilled character impersonator Dan Gates; cosmopolitan Mlle. Marie Duret, making the town a springboard for up-country tours. Though just now offering heavy tragedy and Shakespeare, she returned years later for a long billing at the town's latest opera house, the Oro Fino. Expressing surprise at swift change both in town and its theatres, she presented for her farewell in 1874 that affecting new stage hit, *East Lynne*.

The first roving troupers performed at the elusive Portland Theatre down near the river, known also as Barrell's Building. It succeeded shadowy National Hall and was perhaps that same refurbished structure. Several remodellings are recorded, and a formal "re-opening" in 1857, by the Thomans. Its manager, C. B. Lovell, remained as town stalwart in later years. And here at the Portland, as the fifties fade, a famous crew appears: the Chapman Family, memorable in American stage annals of their day.

The Chapmans, who originated the nation's first Show Boat on the Mississippi River, promptly joined the great migration to the West Coast. Actors all — father, mother, and numerous progeny—their eventful lives belong to its most colorful days. Brilliant Caroline Chapman with brother William were top favorites of San Francisco's legitimate stage when the gold rush was at its height. Restless and talented, they set a pattern for later comers.

It was brother George and wife—the most indefatigable troupers of them all—who headed north for the tall trees. Arriving in Portland by steamer in June, 1857, they were greeted with acclaim.

They drew crowded houses at the upstairs Portland, between side trips up the Valley, to The Dalles and other up-river points. The Oregon circuit had rapidly expanded: Dalles City, then so-called, end of the overland Oregon Trail, was a lively show town. There, in comparative luxury, the Chapmans played a full week, at a forerunner of the later Umatilla House, so well known to travellers.

Portland, easily accessible either from north or south, was a willing host to rambling players. Up from the south came champion jig dancer Mike Mitchell, teamed for laughs with "Old Eph" of the Excelsior Minstrels: the blackface boys came early too. Martin the "Wizzard" held forth; banjo-playing Mart Taylor paused, en route to the Washington wilds. From the north, stage folk drifted down from older Victoria, where the fine Victoria Theatre was opened in 1858 by manager John Potter.

The George Chapmans, dependable if not brilliant players, tarried for weeks. Touring out from town, they played Salem and Oregon City as well. In true trouper style, they shared the life of the region about them. Mrs. George Chapman delivered the Fourth of July oration at Portland in 1857, warmly lauded as "actress, wife and mother." And it was the George Chapmans who returned the next year to open the region's first regularly constituted theatre—Stewart's Willamette Theatre. Though completed as the fifties faded, the active life of this early "temple of the drama" took place in the decade following.

Joined at the old Portland by Mr. and Mrs. Heywood of San Francisco's Metropolitan Theatre, and by other southern players, the Chapmans there staged a series of gripping dramas before taking off for the Sandwich Isles: Kotzebue's *The Stranger, The Iron Chest, The Lottery Ticket*. And, for a benefit, George Chapman featured his favorite role, *The Warlock of the Glen*. Daughter Caroline, namesake of her famous aunt, edged onstage early in *Robert Macaire, or the Two Murderers*. The character acting of the "petite danseuse" drew warm praise. But it was with the presentation by the Chapmans of such polished "domestic drama" as *Rosina Meadows,* the press opined, that "the drama had really arrived" in these parts.

Footloose and trigger-minded, the troupers were on their way.

PLAYERS / and Playhouses of the Sixties

In the sixties, a building decade, the crude log houses, the false-fronted stores of a more urgent day were swiftly outgrown. Permanence was in the air. Stage routes were knotting brash villages into a lively web; steamboats whisted shrilly far up lonesome rivers; business was thriving. The settlers were there to stay, and their buildings said so.

Doggedly, the squat brick stores, the flat mills and marts edged out along Main Streets so deep with mud that local tall tales blandly reported oncoming Conestogas sinking clean out of sight. There was mud a-plenty, no doubt of that. Pioneer life was no simpering maiden's dream. But ugly or not, the box-like structures were solid and built for tomorrow. Even the barest of them flaunted some final curlicue, some added trim to publish the frontier zest for living. With business and transportation under way, in the sixties the theatres came into their own.

First of the Northwest 'opera houses' to rise was in a river town which very early took on metropolitan airs. In Stewart's Willamette Theatre at Portland—the first theatre in Oregon "built expressly for that purpose"—the current exuberance found timely outlet. Opened late in the fifties, its active life spanned the troubled sixties, repeating from afar the nation's dark conflict of that tragic era. Town hall as well as theatre, on its stage the voice of angry Copperheads and impassioned Fenians doubled with Shakespearean actors and romantic spellbinders. Within its walls citizens cried out for street lights to replace smoky kerosene lanterns or muttered protests against the rising tide of "pagan celestials."

The new theatre building—by no means unlovely—gave more than welcome haven to strolling players: it provided a social center for the town. Replacing courthouse or church for concerts, commencements and the larger town meetings, it sheltered basket sociables, stiff formal hops and endless fund-raising "Sanitary Balls" to pay for Civil War medical relief to soldiers. Plus, of course, the growing procession of real play actors now crowding the phrenologists and magicians off-stage. Later, every town of any size was to have its own opera house—a place of magic and of sound community use whose sterling frontier worth is still unsung. As yet, they stood as hopeful outposts in a rag-tag scene.

Edging back from the river, Stewart's Theatre, as it was commonly called, was still conveniently close to the stream's pulsing traffic; to the several wharves built with double levels for flood or normal landings; and to the chugging steamboats heading out for Frisco, for Victoria, and who knows where beyond. Its builder, Charles P. (Speculatin') Stewart, was no niggard, and the new structure seated several hundred persons. Originally located on Stark Street between First and Second, it was later moved sidewise next to Mr. Ladd's brick bank in the same block. Though its architecture followed the prevailing bare mode, a certain distinction was added by the slender pillars, slanted front entrance and ornate portico. With a "larger stage, new scenery, comfortable pit and good ventilation," it swung at once into the town's daily life with gusto, opening November 23, 1858 with *The Honeymoon*. Interspersed between parts of the gay comedy were song-and-dance acts, ended as usual by a brief farce, *Betsy Baker*.

Its first manager, George B. Waldron, formerly of the upstairs Portland, and referred to as a "zealous young actor of merit," played tragic roles. During his several years of direction, various skilled actors trod its boards, along with the inevitable bellringers and professors. Waldron himself travelled both south and north in search of talent, and the convenient coast circuit, by steamer from San Francisco to Portland, Victoria and way points between, soon drew the troupers. Many of them had already crossed the plains by covered wagon, or rounded the Horn by steamer, in the wake of the gold rush.

On the Willamette's new fir stage, still smelling of the forest, the players gave their all to "such devotees of the stage as were not too tired to go, after their day's work of felling trees or baking bread." The plays, varied in type, were in tune with their day, mainly rousing melodramas or dripping tearjerkers splashed with sentiment. Action crowded their rough-hewn plots; their characters were uncompromisingly villains or heroes, and no tomfoolery about it.

But forthright as they were, the plays of the early American stage were far from shoddy. Lusty Will Shakespeare led off, followed by such favorites as Sheridan's *Rivals* or *The School for Scandal*, Goldsmith's *She Stoops to Conquer* or Massinger's *A New Way to Pay Old Debts*. An early survey made within a southern mining section,* showed Webster's *The Golden Farmer*, favorite in the north also, in top place. Historical plays were enjoyed: Bulwer Lytton's *Charles IX* or *Richelieu*. So too were *The Lady of Lyons, Camille, Ingomar,* the spectacular *Mazeppa, The Wild Horse of Tartary* and their ilk. Heart-throb dramas were highly favored: *Uncle Tom's Cabin* and its later romantic rival, *East Lynne,* which in the '80s edged Uncle Tom as "the play most often acted on the American stage." Boucicault's prolific thrillers were popular: *Under the Gaslight, The Streets of New York,* his suave *London Assurance;* arrangements of the Dickens novels went over well, *Oliver Twist, The Cricket on the Hearth.* And comedies rode high as now. Seasoned with a goodly dash of farce or blackface, this hearty fare served the frontier as well as the rest of the nation. Scripts were easily tucked into carpetbags or portmanteaus: the troupers travelled light—and very far.

In general, the influence of the stage there, as noted by Bancroft in his *Works,*** was "beneficial ... When theatrical performances of the better sort were offered there was a marked decline in the patronage of gaming tables and liquor saloons." The rugged Oregon Country responded in kind; its hard-working settlers enjoyed the tonic of good plays. Everywhere along the West Coast much the same players were to be found, most of them, like their patrons, recent migrants from the older East.

Oregon's first "temple of the drama" during its green years was visited by actors good and bad. The George Chapmans returned for extended billings, their changing fortunes eloquent of the trouper's life. Eager audiences could be cruelly fickle. In the Sierra mining camps they had been carried to their hotels on the shoulders of cheering miners; later cold-shouldered as their stars waned before newer luminaries. George Chapman, with much of

---

*Listed in George R. McMinn, *The Theatre of the Golden Era in California* (Caxton, 1941), 197, who cites Joseph Gaer, ed. *Theatre of the Gold Rush Decade in San Francisco* (California Literary Research, Emergency Relief Project, 1935).
**H. H. Bancroft, *Interpocula* (San Francisco, 1888), 268.

fustian in his make-up, called San Francisco home, as did many another mummer. There, during lean years, he presided for a time at the New National Melodeon—a lower-bracket place of amusement so called from the portable organ which dispensed music. And there, in good clan fashion, he was given a lift by the family stars, Caroline and William, billed up-street at Maguire's fine Metropolitan Theatre. George himself shone in such robust melodrama as *The Warlock of the Glen,* or *Davy Crockett.* On tour he was ably assisted by his wife, a dependable actress of the old school, who shared the solid esteem enjoyed by the couple. Daughter Caroline, cast in miscellaneous roles, grew up from the "petite danseuse" to marry a Mr. Nichols in 1862. Northwest stage annals are strewn with listings of the family.

The touring Crabtrees came north again. Travelling with their own coach in storybook fashion, with uniformed rider beating the drum, in the late spring of '62 they enchanted miners in the high Sierras. Lotta, now sixteen, was irresistible in her gay impersonations, her clever song-and-dance acts. Manager was Jake Wallace, expert banjoist and singer, himself a show-stopper in his ballad, "The Days of '49." Details of their wagon tour belong later; here its war-time implications need a word. Legend reports that one of Lotta's lively numbers, marked by a vigorous waving of a Union flag, drew forth "rebel yells" and a near riot.

Legend here has good backing in fact. Like the nation, the Oregon Country was bitterly divided. Oregon's first territorial governor and early state senator Joseph Lane, was hanged in effigy for Southern sympathies. Prisoners were sprung from jail by friends, in sudden midnight raids at Eugene. Joaquin Miller's newspaper, the *Democratic Register,* was there suspended for "sedition." All over the state, the press seethed with angry invective and countercharge: Copperhead, Traitor, they shouted at each other. But in all the turmoil, they were not too busy to note the arrival—by steamer—of the engaging Crabtrees.

Stopped en route by floods, the travelling company, "direct from San Francisco," headed the passenger list of the steamer *Columbia,* on August 31, 1862. Billed at the Willamette for two weeks' engagement as "The Metropolitan Male and Female Minstrels," they were given the red carpet treatment all round.

Headliner of course was Miss Lotta, the Unapproachable, "a wonder in herself in songs, dances and her inimitable Topsy act." As always, the shrewd, proud mother guarded her chick, but this time the ne'er-do-well father, J. A. Crabtree, was along, perhaps for the trip. The extensive company billed also Frank Huston, the Great Ethiopian Delineator; Jake Wallace with his banjo; John Connor, celebrated Irish comedian and vocalist; Mlle. Ella Cadiz, wonderful wire danseuse; A. P. Durand, jig dancer, and Charles Leon, violinist and leader of the orchestra. Prices, one dollar, with fifty cents for the parquette.

"We unhesitatingly pronounce them the best ever seen in Portland. The theatre crowded almost to suffocation," says the *Oregonian* of September 2. Miss Lotta, by now the leading juvenile actress of her day, received "unusual applause." Despite nightly competition from rival artistes at Dennison's Opera House (formerly the Metropolis Hotel) down the street, the Grand Benefit for star and managers, on their departure for British Columbia, drew record crowds. At Victoria and Vancouver they also received warm appreciation.

Lotta's later career is itself legend in the American theatre: the "perpetual Gamin" of the Sierra mining camps who rose to be a luminary of the Legitimate who had duels fought for her; jewels lavished on her—always under mother's careful eye. Plays were written for her and, headlined on Broadway, she toured England also. Quickly achieving fame and fortune, she retired early to a lavish New England villa. A fountain in a San Francisco square marks her affection for early haunts. The virile Oregon Country was to see her again.

By no means all of the Willamette's visitors were hoofers, as, at the moment, were the Crabtrees. Such brilliant stars of the San Francisco stage as James Stark and his famous wife, Sarah Kirby Stark, played there during the early sixties. Stark, scholarly director of the Bay City's Jenny Lind Theatre, often shared its stage with Booth, Matilda Heron or Laura Keene. A prime favorite at the Willamette was Mrs. W. C. Forbes, "distinguished American actress of high reputation on the Eastern stage, in London and the British Isles."

A long billing of Mrs. Forbes in 1860 extended out into the

valley and up-river towns. Known principally for her "unrivalled success" with Shakespearean roles, she included *Lucrezia Borgia, Evadne* and other leading plays "offering a treat never before presented in this state." For her performance of *Hamlet*—her featured role—a special trip of the steamer *Jennie Clark* was run from Oregon City, for those who wished to enjoy "the mimic scenes of the theatre in their highest purity and perfection." Warmly received, she later favored Oregon City with recitations from Shakespeare at Washington Hall, as well as nearby towns.

Succeeding seasons find her entrenched at the Willamette, now supported by her husband, together with Mr. and Mrs. Charles Pope, L. F. Beatty and Miss Lawrence, in a generous repertory. Presented were such dramas as *Damon and Pythias, Camille, Richelieu,* and the fashionable comedy, *The Honeymooners.* Mrs. Forbes, starring as *Bianca,* or *The Italian Wife,* also repeated by request her famous Hamlet. In this latter, to an awed local editor's taste, "she surpassed Macready." By a strange reversal of custom from Shakespeare's own day, many of his most demanding roles, including that of the melancholy Dane, were commonly essayed by women. They were also nibbled at by child prodigies. Notable was Maria Quinn, Hamlet at six.

Members of the energetic Forbes troupe were also exploring the hinterlands, later to be trodden into familiar circuits. Mr. and Mrs. Pope are reported in April of '62 as "leaving by steamer for Walla Walla and the mines," where "people will see some good acting." The tri-weekly steamer *Julia* at that time connected at the Cascades with the *Idaho,* for Dalles City; from there the steamer *Tenino* left Deschutes daily for Wallula, port of inland Walla Walla. Beyond lay Idaho and Montana. Passage from Portland to The Dalles was for a time $5, though later higher; from Deschutes to Wallula $15, with no extra charge for meals. But from San Francisco to Portland, first class fares remained a fairly steady $15, steerage $5. When in pocket, the troupers moved with ease. Under patronage of Governor Douglas, the wide-ranging Forbes Company played the Christmas season of 1862 at Victoria, B. C.

An acid note as to these same players is sounded by sedate Judge Matthew P. Deady in his correspondence to the San Francisco

Bulletin, May, 1862. Observing that "we are not yet civilized enough to submit to the flashy prurience of the modern melodeons" found in southern towns, he adds that "we have endured a good deal of the legitimate drama this winter," with "Beatty, Pope and wife, and Forbes and wife." And, "judging from the recommendations of dramatic critics of the town papers . . . would not be surprised to hear they have been engaged for the New York or London stage." The hard-working settlers, meanwhile, apparently wrung some pleasure even from indifferent players. On the departure of the "stellar" Forbes troupe, a permanent company was announced for the Willamette Theatre. Recruited in San Francisco by veteran manager John S. Potter and Frederick Bell, their ample repertory opened with the comedy *A Wonderful Woman.* Featuring actor John Wood and others, they carried on for several seasons, touring also in neighbor towns as far south as Jacksonville.

A brilliant visitor was the eminent English actor, Charles Kean who, with his actress wife, Ellen Tree, visited the Northwest during his final world tour. Coming by way of Australia, they entertained Pacific Coast towns before crossing to the Atlantic seaboard. At theatre-loving Victoria, B. C. they were feted during an extended presentation of Shakespearean and other plays. The *Pacific Tribune* of Olympia, Washington, of December 4, 1864, contained an invitation to officials of the Territory to be present during the Victoria billing, quoting excursion rates to there from Puget Sound on the steamer *Eliza Anderson.* Portland papers of the same date ran a glowing advance notice of the event, noting that "Mayor Harris of Victoria offers his portly person to perform Falstaff for charitable purposes." Kean's two-night stand at the Willamette Theatre included *The Merchant of Venice,* with the great actor in his featured role of Shylock. It drew hushed and crowded houses despite stiff tariffs and the star's "well known bronchial troubles"—the Grand Manner in acting just then in high esteem.

Fellow passenger with the Keans on the southbound steamer *Brother Jonathan* of tragic memory was Mrs. Frances Fuller Victor, destined to be one of the Northwest's most assiduous writers. Just now, fresh from the East, she was joining a migrant husband in Oregon. To the Willamette stage from the south came poetic Annette Ince, favorite California actress, who at Stockton was presented with a symbolic bouquet for the "chaste purity" of her Shakespearean offerings. Headlined on November 3, 1864, as guest star in Victor Hugo's "terribly exciting drama of *Lucrezia Borgia,*" she held her northern audience "spellbound with the interest of the play." Supporting her were members of the theatre's regular troupe, with G. B. Waldron as Gennarion.

Actor-manager Waldron during visits south was engaged as heavy man at Thos. Maguire's elegant opera house in San Francisco. In its issue of December 31, 1861, *The Golden Era* notes his having "achieved a permanent position by his modest bearing and untiring energy." Though he drew favorable notice there as actor, and later played minor roles on the New York stage, it is as manager that his memory remains green in Northwest annals. It was Waldron who imported for a long engagement at the Willamette a truly exceptional actress — beautiful Julia Dean Hayne, of national renown. From a New York debut at fifteen, she later toured with Joseph Jefferson throughout the South. Broadway acclaimed her in *Camille,* and her arrival in San Francisco for a four weeks' billing at Maguire's Opera House signalled an artistic triumph. It also bolstered his sagging finances in spectacular fashion. Her sincerity and charm conquered all; no actress had received such ovations. Her thirty-night run there set a record, confirming her earlier rating as "one of the finest actresses on the American stage." And this in a day and place where such immortals as Laura Keene and Matilda Heron were in full bloom.

Brilliant and demure, she moved always in an atmosphere of praise, both from critics and audiences, on the West Coast as in the East. The friendly Northwest, during her long stay there, made her peculiarly its own. Billed for long engagements at the Willamette during the fall of the year mentioned, she played also at The Dalles to "rapturous applause," and, ranging far north, to an "immense audience" at Victoria, B. C. Re-booked by G. W. Waldron for the following season, the *Oregonian* of April 6, 1864, remarks: "The Star company of Mr. G. Waldron, with Mrs. Julia Dean Hayne and Miss Frances Goss as leading players, commence a new engagement at the Willamette Theatre this evening. This company, with the exception of Miss Goss, has been with us so long that they seem like our own citizens, and we believe that they have never failed to give satisfaction to their audiences for over a year. The plays for this evening, *Griselda,* a featured role, and *The Eton Boy,* are both good, and we bespeak for the management a full house."

The players ranged far: a month earlier, in February of that year, Mrs. Hayne had appeared at Bannock City, Idaho, and at several way stops. Mr. Waldron's "Star Troupe" also enlivened the fall session of the legislature at Oregon's capital later, vying with the State Fair. Here they opened Salem's new-built Griswold Opera House: a "neat hall, well suited and well ventilated," according to the *Statesman* of July 30, 1864—this modest playhouse soon to be eclipsed by more urban splendor.

Mrs. Hayne's moving interpretation of *Camille* — her stellar role — brought forth the handkerchiefs at the Willamette as elsewhere. As her widening career drew her to the Rocky Mountain country, she opened Piper's Opera House at Virginia City, and also delighted Denver, a player's haven, before a winter season at Salt Lake City. There, in 1864, Brigham Young, staunch patron of the theatre, viewed performances at the magnificent Prophet's Theatre from a special box reserved for himself and wives. A pungent sidelight on her famed *Camille* production comes from here. Oregon papers of the day contain reprints from the *Salt Lake City Union* which record anguished reactions from "Mormons and Mormonesses unused to dissimulation on the stage," greatly disturbed that "the Resident" (Young) would permit so ill a lady to perform. One elderly lady, torn by the star's "shocking cough," at last firmly evaded backstage hands to press upon "the poor sick lady" her special sovereign remedy for colds. Telling tribute to the player's art!

The troubled decade endowed the Willamette with many plays and players. Mrs. S. M. Irwin, of solid West Coast fame, there presented that "finest of French dramas, *The Marble Heart,*" later repeated at Salem. Long runs greeted the timely *Spy of the Potomac* and *The Octoroon,* with Mr. Waldron in the latter "nobly sustaining his San Francisco notoriety." *The Mysterious Stranger* drew crowds, as did that hardy perennial, *Uncle Tom's*

Cabin. Frequent guests from the south were the sprightly Robinson Family, featuring petite daughter Sue, one of the current "fairy stars" so loved in that day. Somewhat less brilliant than Lotta, she was in high favor everywhere, playing also at Oregon City's Washington Hall and all nearby towns. Welcome indeed, for players heading into the vast unknown was the Willamette's dependable stage!

Between billings, its walls echoed to "foaming torrents of oratory" by the war-time senators, Benjamin Stark and James Nesmith. Fiery Joseph Lane and eloquent David Logan held forth there; Olympian Judge Matthew P. Deady lectured on such topics as "Politics and the Public" or "About Words." A succession of eye-punishing panoramas — somewhat lurid forerunners of the modern movies — were presented: Pearson's "Mirror of the War, Paradise Lost, The Wonder of the Nineteenth Century," a "stupendous Drama, showing Heaven, Hell and Paradise in successive scenes." The meteoric Sally Thayer of Salem stopped off, headed out for San Francisco. And, in a dramatic gap, the Fakir of Bordeaux, with "eighteen years of experience among the best Wizzards [*sic*] of the World" repeated his exhibition of legerdemain, for which "the absence of any entertainment of any kind should give the public an appetite." The lively troupers were sorely missed!

The cruel war years which had aged the nation had not spared the useful Willamette, now referred to as "the old Theatre" or "the Willamette barn." Despite remodellings and the introduction of gas, the structure had not kept pace with the town's growth. A fresh wave of migration had set mills and factories humming; prosperous farms invaded the lush valleys; some belated gold strikes stirred the state. Though the Oregon Country buzzed with newcomers, the Portland press bitterly complained that, chilled by the "inhospitable theatre," settlers were being driven elsewhere. A new theatre was needed!

The decline of the "old shell" was retarded by a brilliant Indian summer. In the late sixties, Mrs. Fanny Morgan Phelps, aided by an actor spouse, glowed as bright particular star of the new-formed Ward Theatrical Troupe. These versatile players presented at the Willamette an impressive sequence of plays, among them *Nell Gwynne, Charles the Fifth, Katy O'Shiel* and many others. Manager was Thomas Ward, late of the Victoria Theatre, an able actor. The company of ten, during "a successful tour inland" to Oregon City and Salem, was everywhere enjoyed for several months.

So warm had been their Portland reception that the troupe returned for a longer billing. A succession of excellent plays followed, including Kotzebue's *The Stranger*, adapted by Richard Sheridan for his London Drury Lane; *Don Carlos de Bazan, The Lady of Lyons, Pizarro* (another Sheridan adaptation) and *Jack Sheppard*. A round of enthusiastic Benefits for the cast were given, during which an open letter to Mrs. Phelps appeared in the press. This was signed by many citizens "who for months have witnessed your delineations on the stage . . . wished to show appreciaton of your powers as an artist, and also our respect to you as a lady, before your departure from our city." Here was no gutter artist!

The Grand Complimentary Farewell drew a congested house and a gracious printed response from the lady, signed "Your and the Public's Obedient Servant." Manager Ward also came in for praise—and a Benefit—on March 6, 1866, for "giving good clean plays under unfavorable circumstances"—the company had been prevented from giving a projected Spectacle by the "condition of the stage." Laudatory paragraphs stressed the value of good theatre to the community, in "keeping desirable people here during the winter months" and "discouraging the ruffcuffs who haunt the hells of iniquity in basements."

Warmed by this civic praise, Manager Ward continued at the Willamette for a time, importing a bright star, Charlotte Crampton of San Francisco. An actress of first rank, fresh from an "immense success" in *Hamlet*, Miss Crampton now electrified the north with that daring spectacle, *Mazeppa*. This was repeated for several nights with great acclaim by aid of the "famous trained horse, Roderigo," whose mad flight upstage always froze the spectators' blood. It was a thrilling time.

But the Willamette, temporarily made comfortable for the plays, remained a dingy place, passe' and badly ventilated. Already the young town had its Philharmonic Orchestra, organized that same year; its Library Association was in full swing in an upstairs site near the theatre. A new theatre was imperative! At top speed, work was rushed on an opera house, the Oro Fino, located at First and Stark. It was dedicated on May 30, 1866, with a Promenade Concert by the Fourteenth Infantry Band from Vancouver. And almost before the shavings were dry, its audience moved in with a whoop.

The Oro Fino, though an upstairs theatre at first scantily equipped, was for nine active years one of the town's most popular assembly places. Motley indeed was its entertainment, as were the times. Oratorios, grand balls, minstrel shows crowded each other —even an exciting season of grand opera: a ten-day run by the plush Bianca Opera Company, fresh from "the principal cities of Europe and Australia." *Il Trovatore* and other standard favorites were presented. Outside, the lamplighter still went his faithful rounds, at dusk, in muddy streets, but the little town had time—and taste—for "grand Italian Opera, in costume."

The durable Willamette, however, was by no means spent. More spacious, the larger town meetings and such plays as needed full backstage space were here billed. Notable was an extended run of the renowned Tanner Troupe, during February of '67, in their "Minstrels, Acrobatics and Novelties, from which all vulgarity is carefully excluded." So successful was this that the same troupe leased and refurnished the building for their spectacular ballet-pantomime, "The Red Gnome," the month following. This "chaste and elegant" performance "drew crowded houses and a great many ladies" for a full month. The Tanner Troupe later played in Vancouver, Oregon City and various inland towns. Edging into an honorable decline, the Willamette served out useful years as an armory and museum. Outliving its younger rival, it was finally torn down in 1906.

The bright Oro Fino, or the "new theatre," as it was commonly called, claims a permanent niche as base of operations for a spirited young couple later to achieve some fame. Mr. and Mrs. F. M. Bates, already rated as able actors in the south, took over its fortunes with enthusiasm. Now remembered mainly as the future parents of Blanche Bates, gifted American actress, in their own right both as players and directors they helped to shape events in the new territory.

Young and charming Mrs. Bates had already been starred in New York when the couple joined the western migration. Frank Bates, able and energetic, soon established his own theatre in San Francisco, as leader of an insurgent theatrical group who fought Thos. Maguire's heavy domination in that city. The pair on the way west had served a hard apprenticeship in Rocky Mountain mining camps. Driving to a scheduled performance at Carson City, Nevada, through a blinding snowstorm, two of their horses had died of exhaustion. Doggedly, with an infant in arms, they had somehow pushed on to fulfill the troupers' credo: The Show Must Go On. The West, applauding courage, had adopted them, and responding to the challenge of the frontier, Bates had moved farther north. As the first official manager of the new Oro Fino, he soon replaced its motley by worthwhile plays, done by trained actors. Handsome and magnetic Mrs. Bates promptly attracted a devoted circle of fans.

After urgent backstage change, the Oro Fino during the winter of 1868 witnessed performances of *Camille, Fanchon the Cricket, The Flowers of the Forest* and other dependable dramas. During January, Mr. Bates, playing *Richelieu* to "an audience overflowing the aisles" on the occasion of his Benefit, was presented with a handsome engraved silver cup by the citizens of Portland as a "permanent reminder of many admirers and true friends in the city." The press of the day rings with tribute to his lady.

While further needed carpenter work was in progress, Mr. and Mrs. Bates played a highly successful engagement at the Theatre Royal, Victoria, B. C., presenting *Romeo and Juliet, London Assurance* and similar classics. During their absence their Portland theatre had been given a larger stage, raised floors, an orchestra pit, new chairs and boxes, and a shining outer coat of paint. A quick recruiting trip south brought the acting ensemble up to twelve; in late March a brilliant re-opening headlined Boucicault's *London Assurance.* This was followed by *The Hunchback, Merchant of Venice, Grimalda, Under the Gaslight, Arrah-na-Pogue, Colleen Bawn, Our American Cousin* and other favorites. Warm press notices opined there was "no better company this side of the Rockies."

The presence of Charles Wheatleigh, highly esteemed on the New York and San Francisco stage, as guest artist during April, shed further lustre. It also stirred up an artistic furore, brought on by a critic's fulsome praise of the imported star, with comparisons not to the advantage of popular townsman Bates. Despite such small tempests, the drama was at high tide, with plans actively in progress for a banner fall season.

During the summer, minor players often scattered, to dazzle nearby hamlets with Shakespearean readings or impersonations. Able Mrs. Bates, however, was starred at Maguire's San Francisco Metropolitan Theatre, meanwhile recruiting new talent. Hurrying north in September, what was the dismay of the impatient directors to find the Oro Fino, by some backstairs coup, leased to rival managers, the Messrs. Carter and Phelps earlier mentioned! A spirited public ruckus ensued, led by devoted followers of the popular pair. It was only after indignant threats of boycott and hard-won compromise that Mrs. Bates returned to star at the Oro Fino under the Carter aegis. Mr. Bates also graced a combined Carter ensemble.

The re-appearance of Mrs. Bates in *Camille,* in October of '69, brought packed houses. She later presented *Catherine Howard,* an historical drama; *The Lady of Lyons; The Marble Heart; Macbeth* (with Mr. Bates); *East Lynne,* just then sweeping the boards; and for her Benefit, Riston's *Elizabeth.* A triumphant two-week run at Salem followed, where Reed's Opera House was nearly finished. With the Carter ensemble by now faded, the Bateses resumed management of the Oro Fino under a new lease with an augmented company from the south. Included were Milton Nobles, actor and playwright, and popular Joe Murphy. Both returned often to the Northwest. The town was soothed by a succession of sparkling plays, among them *The Daughter of the Regiment, The Love Chase, The Cricket on the Hearth* and *Nell Gwynne.* Even the spectacular *Mazeppa* was played by their prime favorite, Mrs. Bates, to "prolonged applause."

In the years just following (1871-72) the Bates played all nearby towns. At Dalles City, Mrs. Bates remained a week. Highly esteemed as actors, the pair ranged widely throughout the region, offering worthwhile plays at home and abroad. In 1872, in a rose-covered cottage in Portland, not far from the theatre, daughter Blanche was born.

Inheriting the family dramatic mantle, this well-known player made an early debut with the Frawley Players at Salt Lake City, soon rated as "prime favorite of San Francisco and other Pacific Coast cities." In New York, her lively version of Celia in *As You Like It,* and of Bianca in *The Taming of the Shrew* drew attention. But it was with her hit performance of the Countess in *The Great Ruby* at Daly's that critics forecast "a rising star before which Ada Rehan pales." Her later career needs no retelling here.

In this, it is interesting to note that geography played a role. Miss Bates' most resounding success was in the play written by friend David Belasco, *The Girl of the Golden West.* Belasco, also born on the West Coast, had been basket boy for Mr. and Mrs. Bates at their San Francisco theatre. Reared in Victoria, B. C., he had later appeared briefly in stock at the Oro Fino, and counted the Northwest home. Early ties held strongly throughout later fame. Blanche Bates starred in several of his most ambitious productions. A constant family friend, together with Nance O'Neill, also from the West Coast, she opened several of Belasco's theatres. The tall tree country saw Blanche Bates often. As a member of New York's polished Frawley Company, she played a long and popular run at the New Market during the '80s. Still later, crowned with artistic fame from her lead with George Arliss in *The Darling of the Gods,* she rounded out a circle by returning to break ground for Portland's modern Heilig Theatre in 1910. By then the rose-covered cottage of her birth had long been lost in the city's whirl.

Mr. and Mrs. Bates, plagued by the troupers' itching heel, again went south—and farther. Australia warmly applauded Mrs. Bates. On a return engagement, Mr. Bates, en route from Sydney to Melbourne, somehow met with violent death on shipboard on June 26, 1879. Fading as her daughter's star grew brilliant, Mrs. Bates travelled as the latter's "constant companion and vigilant chaperone. . . . A strikingly handsome woman who played *Camille* . . . and whose dark eyes glow with memories of those variegated sixties."

At the Oro Fino, other managers kept its footlights burning. Durable George B. Waldron turned up from somewhere to guide its fortunes briefly. Reported from Montana in 1869 as one of its favorite actors, he appears later at Salt Lake City, at San Francisco, and finally on the New York stage in support of Clara Morris before vanishing into the troupers' own particular limbo— no press notices. Manager J. M. Carter, freed from the gruelling competition with the popular Bateses, there staged a series of plays, lighter in type. Ranging throughout the region, his company played up-river or down-valley as box office beckoned.

Under stress, the Oro Fino's sagging fortunes received timely aid. Still beloved by Northwest audiences, versatile Mrs. Fanny Morgan Phelps, as its lessee during 1874-75, starred in a succession of plays ranging from *The Drunkard* to *Othello*. Good houses applauded *The Ticket of Leave Man, The Gilded Age, Rip Van Winkle, The Marble Heart, Leah the Forsaken*. And, by no means least, that "latest sensation, *Bertha, The Sewing Machine Girl*," presented "with all the strength of the most efficient Corps Dramatique on the Pacific Coast." The spine-chiller had moved downstage!

Aging rapidly, the Oro Fino had become the haunt of deep, dark melodrama, with the villain in full pursuit, urged on by cat-calls from the gallery. Even before its destruction by fire in 1879, it had been supplanted by that most elegant of playhouses, the New Market.

Beyond the larger towns, the players sometimes had rough going. A hand-written document exists at Jacksonville, dated August 9, 1860, which sets forth that petitioners—citizens of the town—are denied the use of the courthouse for a series of entertainments by one Frank Mayo — "supposed to be of theatrical character." This was the same Frank Mayo, highly esteemed in San Francisco, who played leads for lovely Julia Dean Hayne in Salt Lake City. But, like horse thieves and gamesters, actors were still more or less suspect in odd places. Though Cromwell's decree of 1642, that all actors are "to be punished as Rogues according to the Law" had lost something of its cutting edge in crossing two centuries and an ocean, its dark implications still lingered.

But the once wide-open town of Jacksonville, now more sedate, could at least offer upstairs McCully's Hall to rambling troupers, rather than Taylor's Place, over a stable. The Blaisdell Bell Ringers drew pleased reviews; some stray minstrels and circuses; even a few lectures undermined trade at the flourishing El Dorado bar. At Fort Klamath, soldiers put on some gay skits, possibly home-written. Neighboring Ashland, its only below-stairs hall small and inconvenient, still mainly posted to J'ville for its entertainment.

The drama lagged out on the rugged coast country. Fledgling towns nestled around Coos Bay: Empire City—its name an index to high dreams—founded by settlers from Oregon City in the fifties; Marshfield, just inside the treacherous bar, where a saw-mill buzzed and whined. Tall trees were crashing at nearby North Bend, and from there proud ships would soon anchor in world ports. Prospectors were rocking out gold from the shore sands, but with roads in or out mainly impassable, the steamer from San Francisco was logical for trade or travel. For many years the Coos Bay region remained a suburb of "The City," as it was called. A few straggling players had edged up from Crescent City, where globe-trotting Stephen Massett had noted an "opera house" of sorts. But as in most isolated regions, plays were mainly home-fashioned.

Livest place in the river country was The Dalles, on the busy crossroads of travel. A gold rush town at the moment, its crowded streets echoed to pack trains headed for far places: to Idaho, Montana, the John Day placers. "There wintered miners from Oro Fino and Florence, from Salmon City and Canyon City, British Columbia, Mexico and Australia." So reports, in '64, Colonel Dosch, pioneer builder of the region.* Exceeded only in size by Portland, East Portland, Salem and Astoria, its permanent population of 2,500 was often swelled by transients to 10,000. Gold coins, from one dollar to the fifty-dollar slug, were regulation. So great a stream of the precious metal poured out to the San Francisco mint that a branch was there projected. Prices were fabulous;

---

*The interesting narrative of Col. Henry E. Dosch, dating from 1864, is quoted in Fred Lockley, *History of the Columbia River Valley from The Dalles to the Sea* (Chicago, 1928), I:930.

the river boats made fortunes for their owners; hotels were crowded, and it was either in the dining room of the town's busy caravansery or at the courthouse that early dramatic events took place.

During the sixties, however, Moody's Hall, across the street from the popular Umatilla House, provided a sturdy stage. Ever since the roving Chapman Family began the trek in '58, practically all touring companies had made the alluring trip up-river Famous English actor Charles Kean was among them; demure Julia Dean Hayne was billed at Moody's in '66; later, the Forbes Troupe and Mr. and Mrs. Bates played long engagements. Stray circuses and nifty hoofers stopped off, en route to Walla Walla and inland Washington . . . to Idaho . . . to Montana.

The farther places beckoned. On distant Puget Sound a bustling sawmill town had been born. At Seattle, a former member of the Crabtree troupe, Mart Taylor, had put on the hamlet's "first real dramatic performance" in Yesler's cook house. Older Olympia had paused respectfully for a "reader" in a hotel dining room, in the wake of assorted gymnasts; for General Jack Rag; for 'Yankee' Plummer. Still farther north, Victoria had its lively Theatre Comique.

The vast Oregon Country was splitting off into separate states, closely bound by geography, by common trade routes, by community of purpose. The hand of change was swift and potent . . . Farther and farther, out into the wilderness, the players ventured, weaving an ageless spell.

NEW TOWNS / *New Stars*

For settlers and stage folk alike, the days swung from tall tale to hard fact.

Legend had always hung the Oregon Country with fantastic dream. The Spaniard had there sought a fabled city: Quivira, golden-gated, turquoise-pillared. Cooler Englishmen had joined in a bulldog search for an elusive Northwest Passage, opening trade routes to riches of the East. But though the Yankee captain Gray, quietly nosing over the bar of the Columbia, had sheared off whole armfuls of myth, something of its texture had lingered, even in the drab business of daily living.

Oregon's sky-shouldering trees had long supported bunkhouse whoppers. But by the seventies, droning sawmills were turning out shingles, two-by-fours, ships' knees, gigantic timbers bound for China, Australia, for far ports of the world. Washington was a young giant, flexing strong muscles. Idaho counted herds of sheep between its gemlike lakes. The little towns there had odd names: Boise, Pocatello, Gem. And there were mines, of course.

Montana, behind sabred mountains, had always invited fable. Long after the furious southern gold rush had ebbed, 'explorers' sent there had gravely relayed tales of diamonds in the bare rocks, rubies and emeralds by the hatful: "fields so bestrewn with jewels that the light was blinding." Alluring hoax! But by the seventies, prospectors were ranging tawny hills; the state's pockets were a-jingle with ore, though Butte and Anaconda were magic names for later days. The roving troupers found hard-fisted drama everywhere. But they found eager audiences too, all the more avid from isolation.

In the up-and-coming urban centers, the theatre was pretty well established. In the far wide spaces beyond, wilderness ways still prevailed. Transportation was of course the crux. The little towns were knee-deep in mud, the roads abysmal. Along the Oregon-California stage route, flung out from Sacramento to Portland in the fifties, the mountain roads were often bogged down by fall rains; from November to March the sturdy Concord coaches usually gave way to "mud wagons." Jacksonville and many a frontier town knew far too well the less poetic phrases of *Snowbound*. It was a point of honor, though, for stage drivers to get the mail through. At a pinch, the troupers blew in with the mail pouches.

As to the drama, a certain bravura tone persisted in the hamlets, even though the long-haired professors, the phrenologists, ballad singers and tap dancers had thinned out. Summers, a few travelling troupes in their gay wagons enlivened the scene. The saloons still shed their own synthetic charm: there was action there. Witness a folk ballad written at Jacksonville in those days. It perpetuates a local brush between a Stranger and a Bad Man— and on Christmas Eve. It was no child's fairy tale.

In doggerel rhymed couplets, it tells how the Stranger met up with Black Jack Wilson, who on the blessed Christmas Eve of '63, had shot up Helm's saloon. In the ensuing fracas, James Twogood, stage driver, had been sorely wounded. Casually borrowing a gun from a bystander the Unknown, with deadly aim, had promptly run the Bad Man out of town. The ballad goes on:

> "And then the stranger, who alone
> Had gone and changed the bad man's tone
> Came down and shook hands all around
> And said that he was outward bound,
> And Jimmy shook him by the hand
> An' say: 'In all this glorious land
> There ain't a braver man than you.'
> 'There, there,' says he, 'now that will do.'
> It made the rest of us feel mean.
> His name was Miller. Who? Joaquin."

Joaquin Miller, of course—that tall tale in action! And outward bound as usual. Later to captivate literary London in buckskins and sombrero, spouting ungrammatical couplets from a bearskin rug, he was yet to tackle Frisco in its George Sterling era. The rough-hewn Poet of the Sierras, ever spectacular, may be counted upon to bob up most anywhere in the Oregon Country. His present dramatic entrance is timely. Now remembered mainly for his flamboyant verse, it has somehow been forgotten that he also wrote plays, highly popular in their day.

It was his plays, in fact, that tided Joaquin over difficult years when his townsmen heard his flowing verse with notable reserve. His dramas, on the contrary, struck the public fancy strongly, as astonished Britons feted a shaggy literary lion. His melodrama, *Mexico*, based on the Maximilian legend, was given headlined New York production during the late seventies (1878). At about the same time he dashed off several others, among them his two major plays, *The Danites* and *Forty-Nine*. Produced by actor McKee-Rankin, they drew in crowds during the eighties, where they will be further noted.

At the moment the roving bard was lending both color and action to the scene at J'ville, as the town is still informally called. Its flaming youth somewhat abated, its two most famous taverns, the El Dorado and the Table Rock, were yet in full swing. From gold strikes conveniently at hand, prospectors could replenish empty pokes—the town's main thoroughfares are still underlaid by a mesh of exploring tunnels. Patient Chinese puttered over abandoned claims. But some of the less restless patrons must have paused for reading. The *Jacksonville Sentinel* announced that "Files of the latest foreign and domestic papers will be found at the El Dorado." By the seventies culture was creeping up on the place.

Travelling actors were more numerous and more skilled. There was a stage at McCully's Hall, a solid brick building which survives as Odd Fellows Hall at First and California—the town itself incredibly untouched by time. For larger plays and such demanding social events as the classy Bal Masques, the favorite spot was Veit Schutz Hall out near the brewery owned by the public-spirited citizen of that name. Though Jacksonville had no official opera house during the decade, various travelling companies are there listed: the Boulon Troupe, a favorite thereabouts, in August, '78; the Wretland Troupe in sketches, farces and dances the same month; in November, Morell's Minstrels, "the best Combination that ever appeared here." The Wilton Players presented a series of plays: *A Woman of the People, Uncle Tom's Cabin, The Cross of Gold*. Soon after, the Vernelle Company was highly praised; John Maguire, popular character actor, came down from Portland; local thespians put on minstrels and durable drama. A literary society was formed. The *Democratic Times* of September 5, 1879, states that "Never before in our history have concerts, theatrical performances, etc., been so abundant as this year. Hardly a week passes but we are visited by a show of some kind and the public patronizes them well, though . . . . we are told times are more astringent than ever."

In June of that year Joaquin Miller again passed through Jacksonville, where he had briefly resided. His home town was Eugene, near the site of his parents' donation claim in the Coburg hills. There he had received schooling at Columbia College and briefly edited a paper suppressed for southern sympathies. Now, close to his six-shooter, after hectic years at Canyon City, he carried a thin paper volume of verse—*Joaquin et al*, privately printed at Portland. With him was his young daughter Maude, later to become an actress at San Francisco.

Another transient poet to adorn Jacksonville was young Sam L. Simpson. The so-called Poet Laureate of Oregon, author of a highly esteemed song, "The Beautiful Willamette," was in April of 1880 called south to work on some "neat lines" celebrating the opening of Madame Holt's splendid new inn, the United States Hotel, which had a stage.

Players often skipped nearby Ashland, though a few touring companies tried out below-stairs Houk's Hall; Morrell's Minstrels crammed a rival stage. But as late as 1879, the larger Wilton Company reported "no suitable place" to play. Now-flourishing Medford, only five miles from Jacksonville, destined for swift growth as that colorful town declined, was as yet little more than a dot on the map.

The lush Umpqua farm lands were drawing settlers from Coos Bay. Crescent City, just over the California line, offered an uncertain dock for incoming freight. From here the long swaying pack trains—perhaps a hundred mules with bells a-jingle—would wind in across the spiny hills to J'ville. It all sounded mighty pretty, on paper. And, to the young and tough, romantic. The mule drivers' language didn't count.

At Gold Beach, just inside the Oregon line, fortunes were

rocked out in record time, in the later seventies. Legend as to lost or buried treasure is here permanently imbedded in local records. Farther north Port Orford had a lively day. There was a clot of hotels—sixteen of them—at the site of the old fort, a few crude stores, but no opera house. People were too busy coming or going to sit down. Indian troubles had earlier darkened the scene. The sullen Rogues, fearful of the rising white tide, had joined with northern tribes. Braving sudden massacre and bloody battles, the settlers had held their ground. But fear haunted the lonely cabins dwarfed by the tall firs.

Still farther up the shore at Reedsport, the long shrewd arm of the Hudson's Bay Company had very early planted a small trading post for handling furs. Wild animals were plentiful and their pelts brought in sorely needed cash and supplies. At inland Fort Scott, some miles up the Umpqua, United States troops were garrisoned during the far-flung Indian wars of the seventies. Scottsburg, out at its edge, marked the end of river traffic. Here the jingling overland pack trains from Jacksonville would break camp, whips idle, on their northward way. It was hard to know where legend stopped and cold fact began.

Where trade routes crossed, young towns sprang up almost overnight — some to vanish almost as swiftly, as human need shifted; a few to linger as pallid ghost towns. Names were fantastic: the demure valley monickers, Roseburg, Myrtle Point, Mist, paled beside Alkali, Rattlesnake and Dead Dog of the hinterlands. Few of the struggling hamlets were yet of a size for town halls. Bandon-by-the-Sea and Reedsport pushed out civic bounds, but not until the seventies were fading did stray professional troupes edge in along beach sands from Crescent City to play the Coos Bay towns.

Wharves were jutting out here; regular steamboat traffic, mainly from the south, supported a brisk trade. The huge Simpson mills were a magnet. The upstart hamlets brashly crowded older Empire City, but in all the more isolated frontier towns, entertainment remained mainly home-made. Perhaps for that reason, the few professionals found eager audiences.

A word here as to the frontier audience is perhaps timely. What sort of people faced players across the footlights? Who were the arbiters of boxoffice to worried managers, deciding what fare they might offer?

Seething crest of the western migration was a froth of drifters: con men, gamblers, fancy ladies and assorted Bad Men, vastly alluring to story tellers, to the Bret Hartes, the Jack Londons. The wide open spaces favored expansive behavior, and the resulting 'Western' has ever since retained firm hold on the public fancy. As to that, the renegade was fully present in real life; but, with or without his six-gun, he unfortunately found little time for theatre-going. Nor was the Noble Redman—today highly synthetic —much given to attendance. Neither greatly influenced the dramatic taste of his day.

Transient also, both in habits and taste, were the many miners and loggers who drifted from camp to camp as pay or inclination suggested. These brawny gentlemen played a definite and vital role in the region's growth; in the earlier days of many a frontier town they helped to shape its social patterns. The astute manager, in his choice of entertainment, by no means ignored their rugged tastes, particularly in Skid Road areas. And many a frontier hamlet was little else! Sawmill town Seattle, wide-open Spokane and a dozen towns later to shine as dramatic centers long lingered in the shadow of Brawneyman. He was notably open handed; he loved shows. The trouper, himself a transient, often found the stomp of calk boots and hearty whistles quite as refreshing as the polite patter of white gloves.

Much more potent, however—and far more lasting—was the impact made on dramatic tastes of the region by the deeper, steadier groundswell of "settlers"—the stayers who remained to plow its fields, to build its railroads, to run its stores, and in general to carry on the dull business of daily living. Themselves none too static in nature—they had just completed the Great Migration. Along with Grandfather's clock and Aunt Abbie's sampler, they had brought a fine set of intangibles: beliefs, traditions, ways of living. These took over in the new frontier almost as soon as the dog-trot cabins were finished.

Later travellers, with a nervous eye out for the renegade or the bad man, were often surprised to meet up with hosts obviously on good terms with the sheriff, in some tree-shaded town named

Salem or Portland. In *Yankee Exodus,* Stewart Holbrook has noted the large percentage of New Englanders among the builders of the region. But, whether from East, Midwest or South, it was most often the younger and more imaginative who set forth on the long trek. The innate vigor of the doers followed through. As to plays and players, they were neither uninformed nor static.

When, as often happened, they were thrown on their own resources for entertainment, in some off-beat town, results are at times interesting. At Empire, far up on the Oregon Coast, a Shakespeare play was handsomely mounted by local actors in the seventies, with velvet costumes rented from San Francisco. The same group offered a "French" farce, *Ici on Parle Francaise,* directed by an ex-grand opera singer, wedded to a local doctor. A look at the background of the town is perhaps revealing.

Briefly a boom town awash with transients, the little seacoast village was also home for engineers, officials, doctors from the East in search of milder climate, storekeepers and assorted solid citizens. Reichert's Hall—the opera house to a nest of nearby hamlets, had risen in the sixties. Site of a spread-eagle land development nationally advertised, Empire's wharves had sagged with lumber and fish for distant West Coast ports. Loggers and miners swapped yarns in its crowded bars. But prospectors, headed for the hills on protracted "grubstakes," could safely leave with host John Barr of the Eagle Hotel their entire bankrolls, often running into thousands. No receipts were asked or given. County seat of newly-formed Curry County for a time, its first newspaper was mailed out from here.

At Reichert's there were concerts, stray lectures and frequent plays, usually coached by Madame Towers, the opera singer. In the larger homes, adorned by etched glass doors brought round the Horn, there was a rage for "shadow plays," done in chiaroscuro behind large white curtains. Favorites among these were *Box and Cox* (from the popular farce); *Joan of Arc's Trial; The Hungry Chinaman; The Bleeding Nun; Cagliostro's Magic Mirror,* Schiller's *Song of the Bell,* together with Moving Tableaux highly praised in *Godey's Lady's Book.* Scripts were imported from Boston or New York; their production required careful rehearsal, various 'sets,' gauze curtains, make-up, and colored lights or red fire. For such offerings as the *Witches of Macbeth,* sound effects were added.

The troupers came late to Marshfield, future metropolis of the lower coast country. But it had its own color, and plays were produced by local talent, often directed by some visiting actor from 'the City.' These were the usual standard favorites. Concerts were plentiful; many Scandinavians had come in; there were fine singers, and an active Swedish Singing Society.

Most red-letter events took place in an upstairs rendezvous named Norman's Hall, shrewdly located above a popular restaurant. "This commodious and popular resort for epicures," states the Marshfield *Coast Mail* for February 24, 1884, had "undergone complete renovation." Food was exotic: fresh oysters, received on every steamer, were "served to suit the most fastidious." During entertainments, to skirt the downstairs bar, two entrances "entirely separate from the Palace Saloon" admitted guests to large double dining rooms and four smaller ones for select parties.

Here occurred many Grand Masqued Balls, with brilliant costumes rented, as usual, from San Francisco. These represented historical personages, Arabian Nights or fictional figures. Always a dressy town, Marshfield's afternoon teas took on pageantry. With a large quota of southern residents, as at New Orleans or elsewhere curtains would be drawn at four o'clock, and candles lighted for high tea in formal attire. When some passing ship was hung up on the bar—and this was often—passengers were feted at friendly parties given by the hospitable townsmen.

The superlatives held through, also. The world's largest lumber mill operated here for a time. Its owners, the Simpsons, Yankee industrialists from Maine, lived as largely. Beautiful indeed was the huge home, Shore Acres, commanding the sea, built by the younger Simpson for his bride. For the trousseau, all linen, even for the kitchen, was hand embroidered by a Portland sempstress awarded a medal at the Paris Exposition. For quantity, twelve dozen was not fable. And, as to people, even a lumbering town had its local literates and lofty brows . . . The newspaper was moved over from Empire. There was never lack of action.

Upshore at North Bend, ships were being built—stout ships and lasting, hewn from the highly durable Port Orford cedar. Years later (March 26, 1901) the current *Timberman* remarks: "Vessels built at Coos Bay, Oregon have acquired an enviable reputation for staunchness and durability." The timbers of the steamer *Goliane,* built at North Bend in 1872, bored through, showed "the chips as bright as though the timbers were still standing in the woods." Much of ships and shipping here, of lumber and tall trees, the hum of sawmills. A tang of salt in the air.

Entertainment was on the rugged side: some home-made shows at the Bunkalation—the sprawling men's bunkhouse on the shore at old North Bend; some lectures and concerts at the schoolhouse or the later Pavilion; a few touring players billed at nearby Empire or Marshfield.

The aching lack of professional drama was in part filled by music—good music. Marshfield's Swedish Singing Society went on tour to nearby towns. Madame Towers, the San Francisco opera singer, now living in Marshfield and often heard in concert, decided to give singing lessons as well. Much later, a highly competent women's choral group, the Chaminade Club, attained distinction along the West Coast. But music had an early start. In the seventies the *Marshfield Gazette* tells of a shipment of twenty-four organs, bound for Coquille. Overturned en route in the marsh, they lay floating, to quote its literate editor, "thick as leaves in Vallombrosa." Notable successors to editor Adams, who had written Oregon's first play, were various editors round about. Stayers, too, their pungent comments on events on stage and off undoubtedly helped to form the dramatic tastes of the region.

Easy-to-reach Astoria, far to the north, was a wide-open town in more senses than one. Port of the wide Columbia, rendezvous for deep-sea fishermen, sailors, cannery hands and mill workers, its skid road was remarkable. Valhalla of the drifter, his tastes here were potent. Its waterfront theatre might be the adjunct of some bar from which the dizzy patron might wake to find himself far out at sea. Shanghaiing was a popular sport of the day. Equipped with burlap curtains—and no stage—the so-called theatre contented itself with stray acrobats, tap dancers or some frowsy girl shows. Down on the skid road, that is.

Nowhere were the contrasts in which the frontier delighted more spectacular than here. Up-town, shrewd Captain Flavel in the seventies was building the town's wharves and utilities, together with a handsome mansion on the hill. From its high tower, spyglass in hand, the doughty captain loved to watch his ships, the *Jane Falkenberg* or some other white-sailed beauty, come breezing in from China or "down under." In its panelled music room the Misses Flavel, who had studied voice with Marchesi abroad, would play Lizst or Chopin to slightly puzzled townsfolk. Only the common factor of enjoyment could fuse such opposites.

The town's open door let in the world. Quite early, its firemen's balls, sociables, readings and concerts are liberally bestrewn with visiting artists. Travelling companies arrived by steamer for a northern tour usually got their land legs back by a one-night stand at the port of entry. Home of many races, it had a large Chinese population. A sizable Finnish colony, mainly fishermen, added an old-world flavor to the melange.

Symbol of its cosmopolitan nature was its Occidental Hotel, run by mine host Arrigoni. By 1875, it had entertained "distinguished visitors from nearly every part of the habitable world." The nearby Clatsop Plains Seaside House, a favorite beach resort "with attractions unsurpassed on the Pacific Coast," drew guests from all over the Northwest and farther. There was a Chowder Club at Astoria and a brewery, but also such good taste in music that Professor and Mrs. McGibney and their twelve gifted offspring, later to troupe the entire West Coast, found it congenial for a very long stay. Even after fame had brought long bookings in California and the East, the family came back often for visits and concerts.

Stage folk arrived via the trim steamer *Dixie Thompson,* along with "some 40 daily passengers from Portland." A transient star was celebrated prima donna Agnes Stevenson, "winning the hearts of Astorians with finished operatic airs at Spiritual Hall," the town's first opera house, in May of 1873. Soon after, the "world renowned cantatrice, Anna Bishop . . . assisted by noted musicians," appeared to packed houses at the same place for two nights. This drew a return billing. Listed also at Spiritual Hall in March of '77 is Mme. Camilla Urso, internationally famed violinist. Paris born and conservatory trained, this remarkable and versatile artist, feted in eastern cities, made a long tour of the Northwest in that year, playing even in small hamlets.

Actors were by no means lacking. The Wilton Troupe made a long stay, in a repertory including *Colleen Bawn, The Lady of Lyons, Black-Eyed Susan.* They played also at nearby Oysterville and Knappton, and, taking off for a wide tour of the state and Northwest, were commended for developing in Astoria "a taste for the drama." Senator John H. Mitchell spoke in Spiritual Hall in October, '76. There followed such oddities as Reed's Panorama, after "doing heavy business on Puget Sound," and Professor Lewis' Culmination Troupe, whose "astonishing powers of mesmerising subjects" produced antics highly amusing to the audience. Professor Lewis was also a juggler.

No existing evidence links the unusual name of this early hall with the prevailing wide-spread interest in the occult. Throughout the Northwest, oldtimers report, afternoon seances were as frequent as today's bridge sessions. Prominent personages of the state delved deeply into psychic phenomena, among them that early champion of women's rights, Abigail Scott Duniway of Salem. The builders of Reed's Opera House of that city consulted a psychic as to a favorable date for its opening. There was a spiritual colony at Tillamook; in the daily press, the sensational seances of the Jacobs Brothers at Portland and elsewhere caused heated controversy. But at this distance, the printed page reveals only that Spiritual Hall possessed "one of the finest dancing floors in the State"— along with its huge stage and expansive drafts. In an urgent remodelling, prior to a lease for a long run by the John Jack Dramatic Company in 1877, its name was changed to Liberty Hall.

Captain Jack, as he was often called, may well serve as exemplar of the oldtime trouper. His eastern training, in part at Philadelphia's historic Walnut Street Theatre, was ended by the Civil War, in which he fought with distinction. He later supported Charlotte Cushman on Broadway. Migrating, he was a heavy sufferer from the fire at Virginia City, Nevada. Press notices dub him "as good an actor as a patriot" who "ably supported any character assumed on the stage." One suspects a certain bravura, but with his company, "the most complete Dramatic Company this side of San Francisco," the actor toured the Northwest from top to toe, with varying fortunes.

At Astoria, playing to packed houses, prospects were so bright that he leased the only available hall for a long stay. Under his supervision a new stage was put in and gallery added, though its hard benches remained intact. The transformed theatre—now Liberty Hall, had a grand opening on May 12, 1877, presenting *Aurora Floyd,* dramatized from Mrs. Woods' famous novel. Nightly thereafter for several months current plays were staged, among them *The Daughter of the Regiment, Lady Audley's Secret, Meg's Diversion or Broken Vows, Colleen Bawn, East Lynne* and *Nick of the Woods.* Attractive scenery was painted; the press hailed the clean stage "not only as an evidence of our city's growth, but a gratification to our citizens who require healthy and instructive entertainment."

Bright particular star of John Jack's company was his wife, Annie Firmin, "charming lady and vocalist," and highly popular throughout the Northwest. The maestro, "big of heart as well as body," received due praise as the "distinguished, talented actor from New York." The company, in addition to their regular billings, gave many charity performances: for the Lewiston flood sufferers, for the local fire department. At popular prices (fifty cents or a fish—a salmon was standard currency here) they enlivened the entire summer. When they finally moved on to new pastures in September, it was with the town's "regretful farewells to our portly good friend and fellow, every inch of his 205 avoirdupois a man."

Later that month, the "talented troupe" played at Walla Walla. But heavy weather must have been encountered at The Dalles, where, it is reported, the company was "split up . . . by temporary defection or infirmities." By late October, again in full swing, they played a three weeks' billing at Reed's Opera House, Salem, for the fair. In *London Assurance, Our Boys,* from a full repertory, they rate as "receiving encomiums of praise wherever they have appeared in our state." The John Jack Company were heavy favorites at Coos Bay; they ranged far north to Seattle and way points. Legend reports that at Walla Walla a family sold their only cow in order to witness the entire repertory.

Astoria's refurnished Liberty Hall shortly received the Bernard Grand English Opera Company in *The Bohemian Girl* and *Il Trovatore.* The large cast—thirty artists—drew commentary on the ample size of "our only Hall." There were also Soirees Dansantes,

Billy Emerson's Famous Minstrels, and, in October of 1877, the Deakin's Lilliputian Opera Company of Dwarfs and Giants in *Jack the Giant Killer.*

This unique troupe, which toured the entire Northwest, for water trips chartered the steamer *Kalama.* High praise everywhere followed them and their midget leader, Commodore Nutt. At Salem's Hotel Chemeketa a huge eight-foot bed, built for outsize patrons, was haled from the attic for Colonel Goshen, the giant. At Oregon City, ladies of the troupe rode on the sidewalks in tiny carriages. Eugene billed them in a sash and door factory with lofty ceilings, since doors elsewhere were not high enough for the giant. Here, to shield them, a canopy was run from stage-stop to hotel, and the show was augmented by a mop-haired Circassian Lady. In a return engagement at Astoria, the *Daily Astorian* remarks, "The characters the little actors assume were inimitable . . . They met with unbounded applause. All who attended pronounce it the richest treat of the season." The songs, "novel and excellently rendered . . . compared to the wonderful power and sweetness of singing canaries." The giant was "immense . . . the only fault being that they did not remain long enough." Along the route of the fairy tale procession, photographs of Commodore Nutt and his wife, the widow of Tom Thumb, were on sale, in costumes "worn before the crowned heads of Europe." Such was the motley pattern of the seventies.

Up-river at Vancouver, the footlights burned briskly. The Garrison Theatre — currently Sully's Theatre in honor of the post's commander, stirred with plays, light opera, blackface skits. The post's minstrel troupe, the Pacific Minstrels, travelled to Portland for an appearance at the Oro Fino. When the small barracks theatre burned, the Officers' Club served for awhile. Under Military Items, the *Vancouver Independent* of December 5, 1877, notes that "the old sutler's store is being converted into an amateur theatre, where the histrionic talent of the Post is to distinguish itself during the present winter." Named the Oak Grove Theatre to replace an earlier one of that name, and open to civilians as well, it added much to community enjoyment for several years.

Now, however, the town itself was large enough to support its own hall—somewhat rickety, to be sure, and upstairs of course, but solid enough for the oncoming tide of troupers. Such famous stars as Camilla Urso played in Brant's Hall, just after a billing at Portland's New Market, during her long swing through the Northwest. John Jack and his faithfuls spent almost two months there in the winter of '78. The James Ward Company opened two months in *Inshavogue,* to "good attendance," the Karafly Black Crook Combination shortly after. The Tennessee Jubilee Singers and the Wilton Troupe are also listed.

Civilization, it is said, flows most easily along large rivers, pausing awhile before wide seas or deserts. In the Northwest, the Columbia carried its people and burdens with ease, long before the iron horse began its furious race with time. On its upper reaches, The Dalles, born of river trade, toyed with urban manners. Its friendly Umatilla House sheltered dignitaries from far places: railroad magnates on tour; a president slept there. The roving troupers found it pleasant and profitable to pause before the next hop into the unknown. When fire destroyed both the hotel and Moody's Theatre in 1879, makeshift Lord and Laughlin's Hall did a turn. A commodious place which served also as skating rink and for social occasions, its stage was large enough for a gala production of *The Mikado.* The railroads were edging in. Though gold fields had played out, the last years of the seventies felt a new and firmer push. Hard dollars from cattle ranches and wheat fields replaced elusive gold dust. In 1884 merchant Vogt built the town's first real opera house, in a series built by him.

Other river towns flourished. With the same Midas touch, Hood River turned fruit to gold. Inland Pendleton, a cattle town, mellowed into a busy trading center, its Fraser Theatre seldom dark. Up from Salt Lake City, along the sagebrush circuit, the actors paused to put on make-up where they could. A night's stop; sometimes two. From here their paths led upward—and out.

On the older Willamette turnstile, they now found a permanent theatre at Oregon City, replacing upstairs Washington Hall. Pope's Opera House, built in 1873, despite bare lines, was a solid two-story brick structure, softened by a pillared balcony and the high rounded windows then in vogue. Outside stairs ignored the first-floor hardware emporium; its top floor contained stage, dressing rooms and auditorium—a place of enchantment still green in the memory of living settlers. Here folksy Uncle Tom came to life; Eliza, skirting "ice floes and barking dogs." Blind Tom, a favorite pianist, was enjoyed. Road companies from Portland, travelling troupes from San Francisco played here; the Minstrels, with side-splitting Billy Kersand. Lectures, amateur plays, bazaars, oyster suppers and ice cream festivals alternated until well down in the nineties; when the iron doors clamped down at night, they shut out magic. Wagon shows often visited Oregon City. The aspiring Chautauquas centered near here later.

Few of the blue-jeans towns along the valley circuit could boast a valid opera house. Albany made out with a casual upstairs hall. Corvallis clung to its courthouse for most events until the more spacious Masonic Building took over in the eighties. At Eugene City, the first lean university building, Deady Hall, was achieved mainly by farm donations in 1871. But since the theatre was here frowned upon by officials, it was downtown Lane's Hall, "out by the slough," which sheltered the players.

Lane's Hall, built in 1869, seated some 600 people. Its solid stage, twenty by thirty-two feet in size, sufficed for the usual bell ringers and phrenologists, but famed violinist Camilla Urso also played here. The Pixley sisters there presented *The Secrets* in 1870, in their widening career. The musical McGibenys performed; suave Charles Vivian, impersonator and singer, was a favorite. In slack times, the hall doubled as skating rink, as at The Dalles and elsewhere, roller skating just then being much in vogue. Old-timers vigorously claim the offerings of the day to have been "meaty and educational."

Possible patrons of Lane's Hall could have been Oregon's "boy poet," Sam L. Simpson, who worked briefly on a newspaper here, or his literary peer, the temperamental Joaquin. The latter, who had arrived by covered wagon with his parents in 1853, returned often to visit brother George Melvin Miller. Both were expansive thinkers. Among their grandiose plans were a transcontinental highway stretching from Florence, on the Oregon Coast, to New York City, and various real estate deals.

George's literary wife, Lischen Miller, wrote both poetry and plays. The latter were presented before townsmen who came by horse and buggy to their Fairmount home. She also wrote a column, "Random Remarks," for the Eugene *Guard,* and later helped in founding *Drift,* one of the state's early and transient magazines. Together with visiting cousin Catherine Cogswell, an actress of some stature, they coached Shakespearean and other plays given by the town's amateurs. One of Joaquin's plays, *The Danites,* was presented in his home town by the touring Stutz Company in the late '70s. It was not until the more elegant eighties that rugged Lane's Hall gave way to larger Rhinehart Theatre.

Weary of makeshift stages, players gladly faced the footlights of Salem's new opera house, a substantial three-story brick structure completed just in time to face the new decade. Almost a year in building, Reed's Opera House occupied most of a block at Court and Liberty streets. Though formally opened in September, 1870, a few eager troupes had been earlier billed: the favorite Pixley Dramatic Company in May, the F. M. Bates ensemble just before. As "the only real opera house outside of Portland," the new theatre pre-empted most of the structure's two top floors for its auditorium, stage, circular balcony and dressing rooms. Its first winter season was launched by a full week's run of the Bates Company during the fair. Later, urged by splashing adjectives from an admiring press, nearly all touring companies stopped there. Like most public buildings of the day, it was lighted by kerosene lamps.

Change had not stayed its hand on the larger American stage. Measured by those swinging kerosene lamps at Reed's, the theatre had come far since, in this same town, Massett's guttering candles had blown out on him, evocative though these might be . . . "Enter Lady Macbeth, with a taper" . . . her hands crimson in the half light . . . Tragic, unforgettable! Candles in the fifties, whether in Sheridan's Drury Lane or the far frontier. Kerosene in the sixties, with many a candle still flaming, backstage and out front. Gaslight in the seventies—even earlier in favored places, though the coal oil lamp was to linger on the frontier. Electricity in the eighties, its clear light routing the heavy-mustachioed villains of the gaslight era, completely revising theatre moods and values. Change lagged a bit under the tall firs, even in the larger towns. Reed's, solid and imposing without, was heated by pot-bellied stoves, too often in need of stoking midway in an act. But its hard seats held enchanted patrons. Like the country, the frontier theatre was adolescent, its golden age still to come.

Where trade routes met, to the south, the hamlets were taking on size. At Roseburg, where the southbound stage swayed dizzily by to Frisco, a store had been shrewdly placed by covered wagon migrants in the fifties. The Willamette and Umpqua routes joined not far above; hinting further growth, in '73 the Oregon and California Railway edged in. It also encouraged stray troupers, and here we may catch up with a popular trio long cherished on the West Coast and farther: the Pixley sisters.

The *Roseburg Gazette* of May 14, 1870, notes: "The Pixley Dramatic Company will be welcomed, as our city has been a long time without entertainment." Midway in a long swing through the Northwest, the vivacious Pixleys—Annie, Minnie and Lucy, could be counted on for good houses anywhere. Beginning as precocious child entertainers, they are claimed by Olympia, Washington, as "home town girls," though everywhere beloved. They played long billings at Victoria, B. C., and at Seattle; hospitable Portland also claimed them. Walla Walla, The Dalles and up-river towns knew them well, as did Astoria, Vancouver, Coos Bay and Jacksonville. Sister Lucy fades from the picture early; Minnie and Annie, whether in some lively sister act—say the Shoo-Fly Can Can — or in straight drama, drew admiring patrons. In full luster by the seventies, their tours extended to California and the Southwest, followed by constant plaudits from the press. Midway in the decade (1874), Minnie, idol of local fans, withdrew from the stage in favor of marriage to a Portland business man. Annie, the most gifted of the trio, had married actor-manager Robert Fulford in Portland in 1872, but went on to later fame on the American stage. A hit in the title role of *M'liss*, she toured the country extensively as leading lady for one of the Joseph Jefferson hierarchy, in various popular roles. Returning in full flush of fame to Portland's Casino Theatre, handsome sister Minnie watched proudly from a stagebox.

From the East and south came other reigning stars of the day. But they were actors now, if you please, the term trouper scarcely apropos. And the Oregon Country had become the Pacific Northwest. The players came by leisurely steamboat or swifter rail. With the golden spike safely in place in 1869, the brisk new Union Pacific had flicked off aching miles. For the entire nation it was a time of violent action, of getting and grabbing. Parrington in his *Main Currents in American Thought* sees it as "the railway age," a time of break-up and transition in prevailing social patterns. Stewart Holbrook has well recorded in his *Age of the Moguls* the amoral vigor of its current financiers: Vanderbilt, Astor, Hill, in their brass-knuckled bouts with fortune. Mark Twain lampoons it as *The Gilded Age,* fitly embodied by the veneered schemes of Colonel Sellers. A stage play of that name was to become a great hit on tour. The theatre, always a lively mirror of its times, occasionally subtly molded them: Uncle Tom had performed unexpected feats in his day. And now actor Herne had written a play, *Sag Harbor,* in which nobody ranted or roared on stage. Main characters were just plain people, neither villains nor heroes.

It was disturbing. The Grand Manner seemed curiously off key, the heavy-mustachioed villains slightly ridiculous. The larger towns, close to the singing rails, were first to feel the shift in thought. As the '70s faded, the O. and C. had climbed the steep Cascades, making and breaking towns with ruthless hand . . . Well, that was progress . . . progress!

But what of the silent miles that the train's shrill whistle never reached, where the little towns hid out behind barrier mountains? Would they change too?

WAGON SHOWS / *The Sagebrush Circuit*

Ever since questing man found virtue in the rolling wheel, he has gone farther and seen more, not always to his own advantage. Show business, that lively replica of human living, soon took over the useful wheel. Drama itself meant action, movement. Strolling players had long been acquainted with shank's mare; the wheel was much, much faster. It brought the player directly face to face with willing audiences. In the frontier where vast distances were to be conquered, it was the actor's most dependable friend, if at times his last resort.

Though a few big towns had crept out from the deep forest by now, much of the vast Oregon Country was still virgin: a tangle of slashing fiord and fertile plain. The roving mountain men had gone their way, the lonely trapper outdone by the farmer, the merchant. Loggers were furiously "letting daylight into the swamp." But the wilderness died hard. Here or there, like bright beads on a buckskin garment, the town's flaring gaslight picked out neat patterns of street or highway which only intensified its dark sweep. But beyond a narrow path lay the little towns, the straggling blue jeans hamlets, fully as eager for entertainment. To reach them was the troupers' problem.

Wagon shows of various sorts have always animated frontier annals. Granted, the entertainment they brought was not great art; it was often sheer razzle-dazzle. But the frontiersman was robust; he liked color and action; the wandering show had plenty of both. Before moving into the urban playhouses, now ripe for sophistication, a passing look at gypsy relatives may give back something of their verve. It will at least mark the trouper's progress.

Most striking of the wandering crews which launched Drama into far places were stray groups of professionals such as the touring Crabtrees earlier mentioned. Advance guard of a daring fraternity, their ranks at times included first-rate actors.

As far back as the fifties, small playing companies were forsaking the bright lights of the Bay City, in the south, for the applause and largesse of the high Sierra mining camps. By the sixties, "Wagon shows freely borrowing the names of well-known actors were roaming over the mountains, offering wench dances, a burlesque circus, an Ethiopian act, with a calico party for conclusion. Small circuses were struggling into the mountains with a bit of property, a wild animal or two, a few acrobats. As the season advanced, nearly all the well-known actors of the San Francisco stage appeared in the larger towns. One company travelled more than a thousand miles on foot, playing in a different camp each night." So reports Constance Rourke in her *Troupers of the Gold Coast*. Among such peripatetic players, it might be noted, was young Edwin Booth, learning his craft the hard way. In blackface, and twanging a banjo, he played the negro dandy in *Box and Cox,* among other comedy roles, before giving himself to the more congenial tragic muse.

Players later known and loved over the nation served a hard apprenticeship by stage or wagon, essaying the wilder Oregon Country. As one of them sang:

> "Go whip a ton of grizzly bears,
> With nothing but a tan,
> And prove yourself by all these feats
> To be a western man . . ."

This was the expansive spirit of the day, which could — and often did — lead to fame.

The Crabtree aggregation, knotted about an engaging red-haired mite who laughed as she danced, casually scooping up showered gold in tiny slippers, were old hands at mountain travel. As a child of eight, Lotta had made her debut in the big city's smoky melodeons. Visiting nearby small towns around the Bay, she with her mother had sat out on deck, costumes packed into champagne baskets in good player fashion. There were no cabins, but banjos and baskets could be piled into a windbreak. During the mountain tours, made a-horseback, Lotta slept soundly on a surer-footed mule, the halter held by a rider in front. The careful mother slept but little: crashing boulders, a hasty rider slipping into a high ravine — these did not make for slumber. Yet "scarcely a trouper who rode the trails in those days failed to look back with pleasure to the experience." The lofty mountains belted with flowers, the breath-taking rides from camp to camp, the miners' roaring applause, had left indelible memories.

For Lotta, the shrewd Scotch mother cherished deep dreams of the Legitimate, later fully realized. Just now, an angry pot-shot by the hot-headed father at great manager Maguire for rumored slighting comments on the young star's talents was keeping them out of town. That and the miners' applause. Mart Taylor, seasoned West Coast performer, had taught the girl to dance, to croon a lively ballad, to strum the banjo, himself ceding the spotlight to his talented pupil. And, minstrelsy being to the fore, Lotta gayly blacked up to sing a Topsy song:

"I can play the banjo; yes indeed I can;
I can play a tune upon the frying pan.
I can hollo like a steamboat 'fore she's gwine to stop,
I can sweep a chimney and sing out of the top . . ."

All this in a medley of Irish jigs, Scotch hornpipes, demure impersonations and heart-melting ballads. It was in the best tradition of the day, and whether arriving by wagon, by horseback or on tired feet, it was sure-fire entertainment for eager mining camps or frontier hamlets. Also, with its insistence on stage ease, fine training for a future star.

The Crabtrees were by no means alone in these wilderness jaunts. And there were no dull moments. Lovely Julia Hayne, fresh from the New York stage, along with leading man Frank Mayo, had performed in a southern Oregon mining camp where eager patrons had purchased stools, and staked out places on the floor like claims. The site was described as a "barn." One touring company, en route, had seen its only trunkful of costumes crash down into a jagged ravine . . . So went the days.

It was after several such mountain tours, between billings in town at San Francisco's famed Metropolitan Theatre, that the Crabtrees set forth in their own wagons, in midsummer of '62, for the Oregon Country. Calling themselves the Metropolitan Company, their gaudy coach had its own outrider, to blazon their coming. "They were a convivial company, accustomed to playing together," it is reported. Tall, easy-going Jake Wallace acted as manager, himself an accomplished star. With them travelled Tom La Fonte, versatile master of the trombone — and tested friend of earlier tours. There was also a young lady balladist, an actor named Keen who played the accordion, and a violinist. Mrs. Crabtree, billed as Miss Arabella, played the triangle or gave impersonations as needed. Trigger-minded Mr. Crabtree had been left safely at home. Along the way, "the outrider with his drum wore a cut-glass pin so large and whitely glittering that newspapers in larger towns charged double for hangers and advertising, but the company decided that the effect was worth the cost."

Though details of the Crabtree safari of 1862 are scant indeed, their reported presence at a Rogue River mining camp has already been noted. Here it should be added that their sudden exit followed Lotta's "sailor" act. In this she danced a lively hornpipe, accompanied by the vigorous waving of a Union flag. "Rebel yells and hisses" greeted the latter, but the high spirited girl insisted on finishing her act "even if she were hung for it," according to Jake Wallace.

Other difficulties beset the Crabtrees, attempting to continue over rough roads to Portland. Winter rains had washed out the roads and northbound travel was cut off. The Crabtrees did indeed reach Portland, but it was months later—and by steamboat. Their long billing at the urban Willamette Theatre has been recorded.

Charter members of the wagon show clan were the roving Chapmans, who as far back as the fifties "were on their way northward over rough corduroy roads toward Oregon." The Sierra miners had been captious of late, often pin-pointing gusty applause by brisk pistol shots. Robust though they were, the Chapmans hoped to find less trigger-happy audiences. During pre-railroad days, the number of small companies so travelling must have been legion. Only the brighter names have survived in print, but for years to come the wagon remained the surest way of reaching isolated towns within the far frontier.

Liveliest of all such gypsy caravans was the ageless circus. These West Coast circuses, many of them national in scope, usually arrived by way of the south, where as now they often wintered.

Before the season had ended, they had visited most northern hamlets, stopping as trade warranted. They entered neck and neck with the magicians and readers; the names on garish hangers slapped on barn or fence shouted an ambitious range: the American; the National (Lee and Marsh); the Mammoth. Omitting detail as to their offerings, we may select some few of the more popular caravans which headed north.

Earliest of these was the Pacific Circus, whose stop at Portland in April of '55 preceded even the settlers' home-made production of "Flora's Festival." "They design travelling through the upper country," we learn, "and will extend their tour to Jacksonville and the northern California mining towns before returning south." The Mammoth Circus, two years later, toured the entire coast, stopping at most northern towns, after criss-crossing the nation.

Some of the more glittering West Coast groups were off-shoots of Rowe's celebrated Pioneer Circus of San Francisco; performers there specially trained were duly headlined. Plays were occasionally staged. The splendid Olympic Circus, heading north "after a tour through California," featured versatile George Peoples: "Celebrated Shakespearean clown . . . equally expert . . . as Equestrian tumbler, vaulter, Greek warrior and Indian." From earlier billings with Lee's National Circus, performing at the American Theatre in San Francisco, the proprietors had "engaged at great expense a talented melodramatic company for the production of the grand romantic and allegorical spectacle of *St. George and the Dragon,* or the Seven Champions of Christendom," for the "first time of its presentation by any travelling circus."[*] A pantomime, *Jack the Giant Killer,* met with a great favor on its Northwest tour.

The trail-blazing Mammoth Circus announced in large ads their "popular and Chaste performance on the Stark Common," in the same town, in '57, en route for Vancouver, Cascades and The Dalles. "Boxes, $1.50; Pit, $1.00. N.B.—Ushers will be in attendance and the strictest decorum observed." They later covered the entire Northwest. Barnum himself was headed for Oregon in the '70s.

---

[*]George R. McMinn, *The Theatre of the Golden Era in California* (Caxton, 1941), Chapter XI.

Though we may not follow the circus in later ramblings, it is enough to note that their early forays were usually by wagon or steamboat. When the railroads climbed the mountains in the '80s, they shed none of their spread-eagle brashness in gaining scope; nor, for that matter, their earthy appeal. The Sells Brothers Circus, performing at Eugene and nearby towns in August of '88, mentions its "Great three-ring Arena, with elevated stage; its real Roman Hippodrome," crowning its "five-continent Menagerie; its Gladiatorial combats and its peerless, Poetic, Resplendent Parade." Magnificent, as always!

Early and raucous members of the wagon show family were the roving medicine shows. Using enough theatre to hold the crowds, their main object was of course the sale of dubious nostrums guaranteed to cure—or momentarily banish—all human ills; they had great powers of stimulation. Even the smallest shows carried banjo players, ballad singers or assorted comedians; the major travelling companies, notably Hamlin's Wizard Oil or St. Jacobs, featured trained troupes of skilled performers. The town hall or opera house might be rented for a week's showing of favorite dramas. Such performances would receive due press notice along with scarce legitimate troupes. Many a later celebrity had his start in these roving medicine shows; they were also snug haven for the broken-down trouper.

The weekly *Coast Mail* of Marshfield, Oregon, as late as August of 1901, observes that the Wizard Oil Theatrical Company, "an excellent Troup[e] of players . . . after several weeks of outing at Bandon, will play at Odd Fellows Hall [the town's main opera house] during Fair Week. Remember that they give no Fake show, but a thoroughly clean and entertaining performance at remarkably low prices." The *Mail* goes on to explain "that this company is an organization travelling over the country . . . here for the first time . . . The prime object of the show is to advertise Wizard Oil, but the greater part . . . is strictly first class, the advertising feature simply enabling them to give a better performance for the admission charged." Be that as it may, the gaudy medicine shows are remembered by oldtimers with nostalgic chuckles, and there can be no doubt that they gave a fillip to many a dull day.

On the road, as related by ex-members, summer showings were mainly out of doors. For short stops, the smaller companies would put on their acts from the back or sides of the wagon, with the audience standing about. Many of the wagons, resplendent in red and gold, had roll-up curtains for this purpose. Some were elaborately carved; the performers themselves favored eye-catching costumes. The acts moved swiftly, broken only by fervent sales talks from the pitchmen.

At the more promising towns, a larger encampment would be made. While a hasty stage received a tented cover, a smart dress parade, with blaring band, announced the coming show. In cold weather, some friendly hall might give refuge. Juggling, strong man or blackface acts, comedy skits or dancers were dependable bait for play-hungry settlers.

The big name companies, heading out from the East or Midwest, moved leisurely in their own wagons, billed in the better opera houses. The Northwest was favorite ground. Smaller groups ranged as far north as the rugged Olympic peninsula. There, as late as the 1920s, the brassy razzle-dazzle of the medicine shows resounded: the "high pitchmen" holding forth from the packed wagon; the "low pitchmen" luring patrons from the sidewalk... The scene lighted by smoky gasoline flares; in the background the sing-song chant of shell game artists, making counterpoint with gushing oratory by hawkers; banjos thrumming; a nasal ballad assailing the air; a comedian in full tilt. The city skid roads knew the noisy hucksters well. But so too did far more sedate areas, from the seventies on.

Notable for color and verve were vendors of the Kickapoo Indian remedies, blessed by Buffalo Bill. With a full complement of bogus braves in regalia, reinforced by spectacular sideshows, they could be counted on to liven up a town. The slick shell games usually left the unwary flat; and the wares peddled were quite often some bathtub mixture of common herbs, smartly laced with alcohol. Sold under high-sounding names, they returned fantastic profits.

Somehow the day and age favored nostrums. The most respected magazines, around the turn of the century, sported mammoth ads, claiming incredible cures for various tonics or favorite compounds, aimed at human debility. Eye-popping illustrations make them classics of the spread-eagle school of advertising, equalled only by the fast-talking pitchmen of the medicine shows.

"Healers"— one-man medicine shows — were highly popular: Herman the Healer, "Doctor" Diamond Dick, Doctor J. H. Leonard, travelling in their own wagons, often gave stiff competition to the professional trouper. In his amusing memoirs, *Doubling Back, the Autobiography of an Actor,* Edwards Meade, manager of the pioneer Margaret Iles Repertory Company, tells of pushing north over beach roads from Crescent City in 1901. But, he recollects, "Herman the Healer had been there the week before and taken all the easy money." Martin the "Wizzard" pops up everywhere in the fifties and sixties: in Portland, Jacksonville, Astoria, The Dalles and farther north. The healing was usually effected by mesmerism or hypnotism, with results at times amusing to audiences. Feats of magic or legerdemain, ballad singing or musical acts rounded out the program. Zamloch the Magician and other seers stressed the flair for the supernatural then strongly current.

Much more substantial in their dramatic offerings than these part-time players were the so-called "tent shows" which later invaded the Northwest. Their members, often seasoned professionals who had long followed the gypsy trail, found the wagon or van highly practical in their progress; for this the tent was eminently useful also. Known both in New England and the Midwest, the latter has remained their strongest fortress; there they still deliver rough-hewn drama to rural doorsteps. With their carnival atmosphere, they had made legend; their scripts at times evolving into genuine Americana.

Strongly emphasizing folk entertainment, the tent show steered clear of cities, and, travelling with their own equipment, they were independent of the conventional stage. In contrast to the sketchy, and often rowdy, offerings of the medicine shows, the major travelling tent shows presented standard plays—most often in repertory. This has earned for them the nickname "Tent Repsters" bestowed by *Billboard.* Favored plays were *Hazel Kirke, East Lynne, Lena Rivers, Lightnin', St. Elmo* and *Uncle Tom.*

They were highly uneven in make-up and character, ranging from small fly-by-night aggregations with scanty equipment to massive, long-established companies using many trained professionals. These latter would carry also their own scenery, curtains, modern lighting equipment; even, at times, a revolving stage. Their gay blue and red tents made lively contrast with the staid brown fancied by the Chautauquas, who likewise entertained the nation during the same decades. And the big wagons and ample trucks were right for leisurely travel even after railroads and box-cars came in. Their basic idea—to transport plays to scattered audiences, rather than vice versa—has its own logic, and still holds good in certain far off places.

Backbone of the tent show offerings were the humorous 'Toby' plays, woven about a red-haired, freckled rustic whose awkward antics provided endless entertainment, more especially in rural areas. Distant relatives are possibly William in Shakespeare's *As You Like It,* and Abel Drugget in Ben Jonson's *Alchemist.* But on new-world shores Toby found ample room for growth; he there fathered a whole cycle of scripts, loosely written and enlivened by local quips as needed. The southern Toby could drawl engagingly; in Yankee territory he was shrewd and nasal; in Kansas he was a farm hand; out West he might don chaps or sport a six-gun. But wherever he went, there too went his Heart of Gold. Never the handsome Hero who married the Girl, he was the indispensable Fixer who made all come right in the end. At curtain, he bashfully bowed himself off stage with some light-hearted quip. He invaded vaudeville as the Country Bumpkin.

Original of the tent show Tobies was Frederick R. Wilson, known as "Toby" Wilson until his death in Oklahoma City on August 10, 1952, recipient of a First Citizen award from fellow townsmen. Himself red-haired, with a natural drawl, his playing of two successive roles thus named in offerings of the Murphy Comedians, struck fire with the public. To fill a popular demand, harassed managers became Tobies; whole cycles of sprawling scripts set the wise-cracking rustic in endless tight spots. But in them all, he neatly outwits the scheming city slicker—a potential villain, well worthy of hisses. A recent product of the tent show trail, *Washington Welcomes Toby,* drew both crowds and chuckles in rural areas. Such current hits as *Peg o' My Heart, Polly of the Circus, Rain* were also given.

For the trouper, they provided training comparable to today's "barn theatres." Many a later star won his spurs along the canvas trail, among them Warner Baxter, Jeanne Eagles, Jennifer Jones; others by the way of the Chautauquas. And as to tents, one may note that the temperamental Sarah Bernhardt, feuding with the syndicates on one of her many American farewells, finished the season in Texas under a tent.

Toby Wilson, joined by bandsman friend Joe Baird, moved out to his native West to organize his own Comedians. In this golden age of show business, while urban theatres were a-glitter with stars, the "big top" was also proudly criss-crossing the nation. Buffalo Bill and Pawnee Bill had warm friends among the tent show folk; when their paths met, they foregathered sociably. Oklahoma, Wyoming, the Southwest were good range lands for all; California, where many a trouper wintered. And, in salty renewal, the Northwest, often for annual tours.*

The tented Chautauquas, wagon-borne at times, need their own story. Here they claim a passing word because, in their determined bid for culture they occasionally presented plays, *Peter Pan, The Blue Bird,* even Shakespeare. Education for the masses was their major aim; entertainment was a dependable bait, as with their bawdy opposites, the medicine shows. Bred from the New England passion for lectures, during a summer encampment at Lake Chautauqua in 1874, they spread rapidly outward, soon invading the eager West. Music and popular science eked out the programs.

In Oregon, a major Chautauqua site was Gladstone, near Oregon City. Equipped with a huge semi-permanent pavilion, surrounded by extensive wooded grounds, it had every adjunct for pleasant camping. Not far away was urban Portland, and from here frequent trolleys zinged out during summer encamp-

*First-hand material as to the tent shows was made available by courtesy of Mrs. Pearle Wilson Nicholson, former wife of 'Toby' Wilson, and herself a long-time star of the tent circuits of the region and the nation.

ments. Attendance was often vast: a lecture by the silver-tongued Bryan attracted a record 10,000 extras above the regular patrons. Oregon-born Homer Davenport was popular. For such special events, people came from afar; the everyday program gave outlet to promising local talent. The season's offerings were guaranteed in advance by community backing and vigorous sale of tickets, reasonably priced—a dollar and a half for the twelve day stretch, with camping privileges. The Gladstone Chautauqua, founded in 1893, faded in the twenties.

Southward in the state, Ashland, a pleasant hill town only eighteen miles from the California border, served a wide range of surrounding country. Whole families, bundled into wagon or car, would camp out under the trees for the entire Chautauqua, garnering knowledge and pleasant memories. A fire here wrought havoc to equipment, but the durable cement bowl had lasting qualities. Its friendly circle later sheltered a far more distinguished dramatic adventure, of national import. Here was founded the nation's earliest permanent Shakespeare festival. Begun in 1935, its current lusty achievements are elsewhere noted.

For the upper Willamette Valley, a small but lively permanent site might be found at Albany. Here practically the entire community moved over to its island location for the Chautauqua season, joined by mid-state enthusiasts. And down the coast, Empire, in the Coos Bay area, served as willing host to citizens avid for culture. Here as elsewhere, tents were available for rent; in places, meals were served at moderate prices. Permanent Chautauqua centers, far too numerous for mention, dotted the entire Northwest; from here wagons and tents set forth, until the decline of the movement.

THE SAGEBRUSH CIRCUIT

Beyond the harsh spine of the Cascades, out of easy reach of stage or steamer, lay a vast and lonely land: the cattle country. Here thousand-acre ranches were standard for proper grazing; dawns and dusks blinked out over painted hills, and heat and cold were more than empty words. But, sharply contrasting with green and gentle western slopes, it is as fully Oregon. Here, in fact, if anywhere, the vanishing West still hides out—an unpredictable land of lush bunchgrass, slashed by weird rimrock, with roads climbing at impossible angles. Its settlers must be daring to survive; the men it nurtures feed on daily drama. Shut in by bitter mountains, the little towns were lonely.

As many be imagined, stage drama was scarce in Canyon City, out in distant John Day country, even in the later eighties. The roads were perilous, but some few minor companies got through for billings at Fraternal (Masonic) Hall. Roving bands of gypsies appeared each year for fortune-telling, petty pilfering and 'gibbing.' There were amateur plays. When the press arrived in the nineties, their columns dripped praise for such hardy grey-beards as *East Lynne,* or *Uncle Tom,* put on by the touring Georgia Harper Troupe, or by Donna Vickroy.

Nearby Baker City contributed singers, readers and diverse talent. Baker, the so-called Denver of the West, was an excellent show town, a major stop for companies en route from Salt Lake City out along the sagebrush circuit. Exemplar also of the boom or bust psychology then rampant, which made frontier hamlets ghost town or metropolis by sudden whim of gold strike or railroad. Its cross-state stance profited by both, aided by real estate flurries. It had large ideas, and its grandiose Rust's Opera House was favorite with players. Pendleton, to the west, which had built its Fraser Opera House in 1886, was likewise a good show town. Settled by midwestern plains folk who thriftily exchanged sod homes for mansions, it had survived floods and Indian troubles to wax prosperous on grain and cattle. Its busy opera house saw many plays, and the town's dramatic flair lingers in its famed annual Round-up and rodeo featuring an impressive night show: the Happy Canyon pageant.

The mountains resisted travel, but La Grande offered a neat opera house to such stray companies as might stop. Here young Maude Durbin, wife-to-be of Otis Skinner, following her parents west, launched a promising dramatic career. Angling north and west, the sagebrush circuit tapped The Dalles and Walla Walla, ready show towns both, and Spokane, avid for theatre and center of Washington's rich Inland Empire. Touring professionals were warmly greeted, but well down in the present century, wagons still figured in their progress.

Such rugged terrain sorely tried the troupers' mettle. A light-hearted account of the trials of roving repertory groups is that left by trouper Ed Meade (born Edwards Hoag). His adventures with the wagons enlivened several years at the turn of the century. They carried him thousands of miles, from Canada to California, out through the Northwest's most remote back country, along its winding coast, as actor, manager or zestful driver of a two or four horse team. This after conventional stage training: handy man for the Alba Heywood Company (at $15 a month and cakes); super for Louis James; training at the Boston Lyceum, and travelling professional, mainly in impersonations of Bill Nye, approved by that notable. After successful years of touring the Midwest, we may take up with him at far-away Saskatchewan where, stranded, he was rescued by a prosperous member of the tent show family, Robert Buchanan, just then touring the north with private car, brass band and "canvas opera house," presenting plays in repertory.

The rags-to-riches life of the 'repsters' appears: with the "jolly crew of actors" travelled also a cook and porter, canvas men and stake drivers, scene shifters and property men, the latter doubling in brass for parades. But, after a highly successful series of weekly stands, winter overtook them at Calgary; the plush private car existence gave way to draggled journeys around the province. At one stop, in a railroad roundhouse, the audience of Blackfeet Indians "could not understand the plays, but enjoyed the knife fights and the music." By welcome contrast, Vancouver and New Westminster offered urban theatres and audiences.

Back on American soil, Meade was successively member of the touring Alcazar Stock Company from San Francisco, just then playing at Seattle's old Third Avenue, a vaudeville troupe, doing two turns a day, and an *Uncle Tom's Cabin* company, with its "bloodhound" actors. With Meade doubling as either Uncle Tom or Little Eva, this jaunt ended abruptly "because he could not do the bloodhound." Quitting in Spokane with $5 in his pocket and the temperature twenty below zero, a lucky meeting with old friend Robert Buchanan changed his whole fortune—thanks to the wagons.

Presenting stage durables in smaller towns with a bright new company, they were told at Weiser, Idaho, by a travelling salesman about a "wonderful town named Burns, in Oregon, situated 150 miles from the railroad. If we could get a small company together, go to Burns and play for a week, we would make more money than we could spend." Burns, out in the sagebrush near Bill Hanley's Bell A ranch, was "a wild and woolly wide open stock town" which "also contained a great many refined, cultured, wealthy and talented people." It could be reached only by dizzy stage roads through steep mountains, but the daring company set forth: five men, two women and a boy—all that remained of a big show of twenty persons, band and orchestra.

Meade's adventures as advance agent, billing tiny mountain hamlets, were breath-taking, but so were results. With the stage hooked on to four horses they climbed the mountain to Burns, where, by active doubling, they were able to present a dozen plays in repertory. "What we really needed was not more plays, but more wigs." The audiences of cow punchers, cattle men and settlers were free-handed and appreciative. The company "did a wonderful business" and, pushing north by stage to Canyon City and Sumpter, they reached Weiser by rail, where the Buchanan private car had been left with the cook.

So successful, both as to finances and health for the troupe, had the foray been that the manager sold the private car at Boise to buy wagons. In these, 2,000 miles of mountain road were negotiated during the summer — through Idaho, Utah, Nevada and California, and "keeping clear of railroad towns till we reached Elkton, Nevada by the time it was too late to travel by team." Mining and cattle towns along the way eagerly applauded *The Two Orphans, East Lynne* and such rock-bound favorites.

With his own company, the Southern Stock Company, Meade continued the wagon tours for years, though by 1901 railroads had connected all the larger towns. Mountain hamlets "that had not seen a good dramatic show for years" were the main objective. At Lakeview, Oregon, the company adorned the year's most festive occasion: the big five-day Fourth of July celebration, which added horse racing, broncho busting, Indian war dances and sheep shearing contests. "The opera house was over a stable where people purchased four feet of space for a reserved seat and furnished their own chairs." Packed houses proved that "townspeople in small places enjoyed shows."

Nearby Linkville (Klamath Falls), with 600 inhabitants, had a real opera house, though its genial manager, John V. Houston, was ill in San Francisco. Continuing by mountain roads to Ashland, Medford, Jacksonville and Grants Pass, their company was augmented by professionals from Portland.

Oregon's isolated coast towns welcomed the wagons. Playing at Crescent City's eighteen-year-old Endart Opera House, fire struck during the night, completely destroying theatre, scenery and wardrobes. Renting a small dance hall, they built a plank stage and seats, "painted diamond dye scenery and, furnished with costumes and grease paint by the local amateur club" drew overflow houses for another two nights.

The coast agreeably combined business with vacations. Such favorite hostelries as Bedallion's or Blanco's offered wonderful seafood. Here, in the creaky opera house over Gross Brothers, main families of the town held down front seats, reserved; behind them sat sundry hotel guests, the life-saving crew, the river steamboat men, the logging and sawmill employees and their families. Gold Beach and Port Orford were likely stops; en route they had presented *East Lynne* at Myrtle Creek's three-story opera house. They vowed more permanent return to friendly Marshfield . . . And so back along coast roads to San Francisco by way of Crescent City, where they again played to banner crowds at Endart's New Opera House, swiftly rebuilt.

Two teams now instead of one, with extra horse for steep pulls. And life was never dull: rampaging cowboys occasionally shot up a show; Fort Bidwell was nearly deserted by a gold strike reported by sheepherders in the hills. At Silver Lake, Oregon, where the town hall had just burned, they played *The Fatal Wedding* in an empty barn with long stalls and hay-covered floor, "to the accompaniment of much sneezing from the audience." But so successfully that *Old Kentucky, Black Bess* and other favorites were demanded. First productions at Fort Klamath had been "to well educated and well behaved Indians." In the sagebrush reaches around Prineville and Wagontire where ever-present feuds were

/69

promptly settled by six-gun, stage action at times seemed a trifle pale.

In the green and peaceful valley towns, Eugene or Corvallis, managers might disband their troupes, themselves heading back for a final fling in the wide spaces with the Georgia Harper Players or other roving actors, before settling down for the winter in Frisco, that players' paradise. From here, in 1905, as manager for the talented Margaret Iles, Meade's career entered a new and wider phase.

The touring company bearing her name successfully played the larger northwestern towns, moving by rail or steamer as needed. The star herself was briefly lured east, to play stock with Constance Crawley in New Orleans and the Midwest. When the West called again, she joined forces with Manager Meade and good friend John Houston, opening in the latter's "kerosene circuit" with a strong company. Largely through Houston's efforts, Klamath Falls became a favorite stop for touring companies. When his opera house burned, he promptly built another, where the town's amateur efforts were also sheltered.

The popular Margaret Iles Company was warmly rewarded along the sagebrush trail. At Lakeview, where the livery stable opera house had been replaced by a much more splendid one with full stage, scenery and Grand Rapids opera chairs, a thousand dollar guarantee check for a week's playing was left uncashed by the happy company. Behind a four-horse team, they explored the mountain counties of northern California, returning by way of Drain, Scottsburg, and Reedsport to the favorite coast rendezvous. Over hard beach sands by wide-tired wagons, they played for weeks at Marshfield.*

Rival companies now cluttered the scene. The pioneer Iles Company, purchasing a huge coach and four from a retiring stage company, in 1909 covered Plumas, Lassen and Modoc counties of California, together with Klamath, Lake, Grant and Crook counties of Oregon. The thrill of driving four horses from fourteen to fifty-four miles daily engrossed the manager. Their 1910 season ranged from fair week in cow country to the salty beach towns

---

*Edwards Hoag Meade, *Doubling Back, the Autobiography of an Actor* (Chicago, 1916), 150.

of Coos Bay, with the valley cities in stride. This time, after the long safari, the company went into stock in November, at the Bijou Theatre, Walla Walla. There Margaret Iles, a favorite in this show-loving town, played a long season. Only the sudden illness of Manager Meade ended his exciting forays into the mountain and sagebrush country of the Northwest.

The service of the wagon to the acting profession has by no means ended. Its modern version—the motor van—carries actors and their equipment to waiting audiences with ease and directness, throughout many rural areas of the nation. The Black Hills of Dakota, remote areas of the South and New England know them well. In the Pacific Northwest, a few years back, the Washington State Touring Theatre employed mobile units to good effect, as had many before them. Idaho's Virginia City Players, reviving oldtime melodrama, rode the stage to the smaller towns. St. Martin's College, presenting their *Miracle of Fatima,* found the wheel indispensable in transporting their huge cast, made up of men, women, children and various animals. Rough and ready theatre, perhaps, but with its own benison for the lonely places.

Meanwhile, in sleek urban playhouses, curtains were rising on far more sophisticated scenes.

RED PLUSH / *and Progress*

Theatres, like people, have their ups and downs, their dazzling moments, their slow decay. And theatres, more than most buildings, take on color from their times. So with an old playhouse standing on a quiet by-street near Portland's waterfront, shoulders still squared to wind and sun. Ranking in its day as the Northwest's handsomest theatre, its story has in it something of fable. Its frame, tough as a hickory sapling, stands knee-deep in reality: it got its sinews from hard-fisted builders.

Wilderness ways are hard ways. By the time their first flimsy playhouses had lost their paint, settlers in the Oregon Country were beginning to hanker for creature comforts, for remembered ways of living. Feet planted in new soil, they had built feverishly, and, as the seventies faded, they could rest a spell. The frontier had taken to the hills.

Within the theatre, too, there had been change. The barnstorming troupers were seasoned thespians now; the slapdash halls, chilly and drafty, were outmoded. The strolling players, knotted into suave companies, craved elbow room and some permanence for their magic craft. The settlers, with more leisure, were building in brick and stone. In answer to strong public need, the glittering New Market, Portland's playhouse of its red plush era, arose to take the spotlight.

And high time, too! The old Oro Fino, hastily flung together for its opening in 1866, from a dozen years of shuffling boots was dingy and forlorn. Melodrama stalked its boards: *Bertha, the Sewing Machine Girl, or Death at the Wheel; Ten Nights in a Barroom,* the Great Moral Drama. (Beer was served downstairs!) The earlier Willamette (Stewart's) Theatre, Portland's pioneer theatre of the sixties, was a drab armory and museum, where an occasional hoofer or lecturer held forth. Later (1875) someone opened a minor theatre, the Adelphi, in the Oro Fino block, for variety shows mainly. But there was sawdust on the floor! The maturing Oregon Country yearned for less homespun backgrounds.

Only the hardy temper of the troupers had kept them going. Patrons squirmed on hard seats; players shivered in drafty halls. The sprawling river town was growing up. Steamboat day drew milling crowds. There were long blocks of business structures, edging out toward the hills, with new-fangled gaslights. River transit was by chugging ferries, with steel bridges still in the offing. But there were streetcars now — horse-drawn, bearing patrons out to comfortable homes along the Heights. The frontier had been open-handed with its men of action. Every five minutes a bob-tailed car jogged past the downtown hotels: the Clarendon, the Cosmopolitan, the Occidental . . . Progress, by George, and only thirty years up from scratch! As to the new theatre, it was a man of action who took that little matter in hand. No sleazy wooden firetrap this time! Brick and stone fully reflected the new mood, to catch up with the nation.

Remembered by oldtimers as the most glamorous of Portland's early playhouses, there was good reason for the New Market's lasting spell. Larger and stronger than its hasty forbears, there was grace in its firm lines as well. Down the street a way, the new Ladd and Tilton bank had set the pace handsomely; an urge for permanence in its sturdy two-story brick frame; a bid for beauty in its iron grilles, its "pilasters on Doric bases, with Corinthian columns;" its interior "furnished with lavish elegance."

Builder of the aspiring structure was Alexander P. Ankeny, captain of industry, whose restless energy helped to hew the city from the tall trees. A Pennsylvania riverman transplanted from Virginia, he followed the California gold rush overland in '49, and pushing north from there landed in Portland two years later. Immediately he plunged into the seething activity of the raw frontier town. He became interested in the Wells, Fargo Express; engaged in real estate ventures; in gold mining and the lumber business.

"Through the successful conduct of these various lines of industry," we read, "he became the possessor of a substantial fortune. Whatever he undertook, he carried through, and knew no such word as fail." Primarily, Captain Ankeny was a steamboat man, as part owner of the pioneer river boats *Wasco, Independence* and others. He also helped to open a pack trail to the eastern Oregon gold mines via the Columbia Gorge—later to become the Columbia River Highway. But he was a shrewd merchant as well. With his sons, Levi and Henry, he established the firm of Ankeny and Sons, serving the Northwest for many years. Renamed for him, Portland's Ankeny Street marks his efforts in building up its mercantile district. Though the New Market was but one of several ventures (later he traded it for a gold mine) it was built, like his own mansion, definitely in the grand manner.

For the opening of the new theatre (March 24, 1875), a red-letter night in Portland's annals, the town turned out in its Sunday best. "The men in their cowhide boots and tall hats are very gallant to their bemittened and bebustled ladies," we learn. Statuary, chandeliers and upholstery had been ordered from the East, and weeks spent in placing them. A drop curtain, forty by sixty feet in size, painted at a cost of $400, showed an exotic Mediterranean scene; there were numerous sets and flats backstage. All furnishings were in the same lavish mood.

The theatre's opening had been delayed by the financial panic of '73, construction of the building having run its owner well up into the five-numeral bracket. Its framework, however, was completed the previous year, and the downstairs markets in their arched stalls put into full swing. For the long-deferred opening night of the theatre, anticipation ran so high that a local newssheet suggested auctioning seats, at sky-high prices. Captain Ankeny himself scuttled such an unfair plan. When the northbound steamer *Idaho* at last reached town, bearing noted actor James A. Herne and his large company, its shrill whistle signalled a very memorable curtain for the Oregon Country.

"Entering the new theatre with the gay crowd," a later critic records, "we find commodious boxes on each side of the stage. Around the parquet with its horseshoe circle are long red plush benches." Prices for the opening night were held to $1.00 for the balcony, $1.50 for the parquet. Boxes for the town's elite were of course higher—from $4.00 to $7.50. Local journals noted "the refined and appreciative audience which crowded the new and popular place of amusement, able to seat 1200 people; stage and auditorium presented a scene of dazzling brilliance under the glamour of a hundred gas jets, the like of which has never before been seen in this city." It was, in fact, "bewildering to the senses."

The crowd liked the play—*Rip Van Winkle;* the scenery was complete and perfect in its working (except for some creaking); the next play, *Kathleen Mavourneen,* was in rehearsal. Great plans were afoot, and a prosperous year for the new theatre foretold.

A cosmopolitan air was added by a third-floor cafe, reached by separate entrances from the street below. These served the theatre as well, and there were stairways between floors, so that patrons of the downstairs marts could enjoy a Saturday matinee at pleasure. The theatre proper took up most of both the second and third floors of the building; the stage was sixty by one hundred and forty feet in reach, with an ample thirty-five foot ceiling. There was a full balcony and orchestra, set off by roomy boxes, all dressed in the prevailing sumptuous red plush. Stage equipment was excellent for its day. Extra scenery was hoisted up from below from a twenty-foot alleyway, used also for driving wagons in and out of the luxurious market. With its marble counters and rows of arched stalls, nothing like it had ever been seen in the Oregon Country.

At the theatre's opening, Actor Herne delighted his audience in the role made famous by a succession of Joseph Jeffersons. A "grand orchestra" gave forth with selections; added was a Silver Clog, between acts. Herne, of whom we shall hear more later, stayed at the New Market a full month with his company. They presented, by aid of local actors, a series of favorite offerings, among them *Dombey and Son, The Clockmaker's Hat, Oliver Twist, Handy Andy* and the perennial *Rosina Meadows, or City Temptation Uninvited.*

From the first, the theatre had its ups and downs, as did the players. Actor Herne, drawing crowded houses in *Rip,* three times repeated, was less warmly received in other roles. Or was it the plays which were threadbare? At times the "beautiful temple of the drama" was only partly filled. At month's end, pushing into newer pastures up in the Puget Sound country, Herne took with him most of his company. There remained, however, those local professionals who had enlarged his acting group—seasoned players who between town billings had toured out to Astoria, Marshfield or up the Valley circuit. Among these were actor Robert Fulford and his later famous wife, Annie Pixley and her sister Minnie. In an uncertain interim, while Levi Ankeny combed San Francisco for new talent, Mrs. Fulford was featured in a series of plays climaxed by Wilkie Collins' *The New Magdalen*. As director, versatile and energetic Mrs. Fanny Morgan Phelps took over.

This able lady, who returned from the Sound country as "manageress and lessee" of the fine new theatre, not only managed to fill it nightly but to draw down compliments from the critics in practically any role undertaken. Under her management, for a week's run in July of 1875, was listed the "world-renowned Lingards, with a complete Dramatic organization," in "person-ations and the beautiful play *La Tentation*" (Mrs. Phelps in the cast). This shrewdly coincided with the "first Moonlight Excursion of the Season given by the City Rifles on the large and commodious steamer, Annie Stewart, with beautiful barge Autocrat. Brass and String Band. No Spirituous Liquors Sold." The Phelps Company also presented *Uncle Tom's Cabin, Our Country Cousin* and *The French Spy*. Actor Herne, drifting back from the north in the fall, played the lead in *David Garrick*, with Mrs. Phelps assisting.

There was grand opera, too. Levi Ankeny, on his trip to San Francisco, had there engaged a visiting operatic troupe for a full Christmas season. Sung by eminent artists, *Il Trovatore, Ernani, La Traviata* and *Lucia* saluted the infant years at the New Market, and the town crowded its handsome new opera house for these. For the next several years its playbills mirror the swift change in local backgrounds as well as in the national scene. During the dozen years of the theatre's most active life, the river village mushroomed from a town "well past the 10,000 mark" to a "city of some 40,000 souls." Eminent players trod its boards. The queenly New Market saw her fading rival, the Oro Fino, lapse into dingy oblivion before its destruction by fire in 1876.

Builder Ankeny, on the contrary, had determined that his theatre should be—and remain—a first-class place. A yellowed set of rules for the New Market Theatre re-creates the times. The use of "kerosene, coal oil or other burning fluids for light" (only candles and gas allowed) is strictly forbidden. "All persons other than those belonging to the troupe" are banned from the stage, with careful rules as to entrances and exits of others from both stage and building. Incidentally, "All gentlemen who use tobacco will be particular to use the spittoons in order to ensure cleanliness on the stage."

Billed during this period were Robert Fulford in *Hamlet* (July, 1877); Rose Eytinge in *The Hunchback* and *East Lynne;* Primrose and West's Minstrels (1879); Captain Jack Crawford of the Black Hills in a shooting exhibition. A succession of brilliant events relieved the hodge-podge offered for groundlings. During the appearance of Frank Mayo in *Davy Crockett,* Portland first learned the meaning of the magic symbols S.R.O. The town's blood pulsed warmly in its veins.

The handsome opera house also found space for civic events: commencements, the first concert of the Portland Orchestral Union in February of '82—forerunner of its later symphony. Music had always been favored; light operas were becoming the rage, and almost anything in this category could be counted on for a full house. With San Francisco only a step away, famed singers and stage notables added the short trip north to try out the plush New Market. From here on listings of the two coast cities are largely the same. And it was not only the troupers who travelled. For civilians as well, the "trip to Frisco" was a favorite jaunt.

It was in these lively days when sophistication elbowed the homespun, that dinner jackets and formal dress became standard at the New Market. An amusing incident impales the spirit of the times. During the life of the theatre, several competent managers guided its fortunes. One such, Mr. F. M. Stechhan, taking over from the iron-willed Mr. Ankeny, became as well the glass of fashion for the town's younger set. This dapper individual had brought up from the south a glamorous opera troupe, billed in Gluck's *Orpheus and Eurydice.* Since its "grand ballet" was a major attraction, a local newspaper playfully suggested that "the bald-headed row will no doubt occupy front seats." But the town for some reason boasted few bald-headed men; a group of young bloods considered the crisis. Just before curtain time, twelve bald-headed men, each in faultless evening attire, filed separately into the theatre. Each carried a small bouquet, and each was apparently oblivious of the others. Ushered prominently into the front row, the dozen gleaming bald pates were "as much the cynosure of all eyes as the scantily clad performers." The more so when at a "preconcerted signal" the twelve men arose, and "levelling bouquets at the esprit de corps de ballet," showered the stage with flowers, amid chuckles from the audience. Later, when the pranksters arose to pull off their wigs in obeisance to the prima donna, certain social scions were recognized. But not before they had stolen the show.

. . . Such was life in the elegant eighties. From afar, the frontier theatre mirrored the maturing scene beyond. On the New Market's stage, at its zenith, appeared such national favorites as William Gillette in *The Private Secretary* and *The Rajah* (August, 1885); Frederick Warde in *Richard III* and *Virginius,* earlier that year; Lawrence Barrett and Louis James; Denman Thompson, Louise Kellogg, to name but a few. Emma Abbott, prima donna billed at the New Market during its latter days, sang often at other Portland theatres and owned property in the town. Scarcely a major star is missing. Among them a few reversed the traditional course assigned to the star of empire.

One such was David Belasco, who prepared for later fame and fortune by useful apprenticeship on his native West Coast. The clerical collar he always wore was loving reminder of early training in a Catholic boys' school in Victoria, B. C.; nostalgic memories of his California days haunt many of his plays, notably his well-known *Girl of the Golden West,* which inspired Puccini's opera of that name. For important leads he chose old friends Blanche Bates or Nance O'Neill, who also christened many of his new theatres. The bond was more than sentimental. He had barnstormed widely out there, playing stock in towns large and small. San Francisco had nurtured his budding talent, when at nineteen he was stage director at Maguire's Theatre. With James A. Herne he had there collaborated on an early play, *Hearts of Oak.* At Portland's New Market he later acted in and produced his own play, *May Blossom.* There his brother Fred had for a time managed the Belasco Theatre, earlier the Columbia. The hard-hitting West may well have sharpened the edge of his later realism.

The New Market's splendor did not remain unchallenged. Flushed with prosperity, other northern towns ran up new opera houses, brave with plush. The more ornate big-town theatres in general date from the nineties, but elsewhere there had been beginnings. The Dalles, bustling trade center for the upper river country, had tired of pinch-hitters for its Moody's Hall, destroyed by fire. The town's first real opera house was built in 1884 by Maximilian Vogt. Devoted patron of the arts, he did not grudge money spent for their enjoyment.

Vogt's first opera house—he was to build several—was a solid two-story brick structure equipped with good stage, drop curtain and painted flats. Conveniently close to the river, it welcomed roving troupers, out for the river jaunt. Skilled performers now faced its footlights, ranging from the serene Fisk Jubilee Singers to noisy circus crews on an annual tour. Local thespians stormed onstage in *Queen Esther,* an oratorio. In the thrifty custom of the day, Vogt's was an upstairs hall, with drugstore underneath. Though small, seating only 300 patrons, it operated so profitably that its owner decided, as the eighties faded, to build a larger one farther uptown.

Lusty Astoria, down at the river's wide mouth, was another good show town. As the eighties dawned, John Ross, city clerk, decided to build a proper theatre well uptown, to replace drafty waterfront Liberty Hall. The Ross Opera House, seating 2,000 people, had good acoustics and modern equipment. Its stage was said to be the deepest on the coast. A built-in balcony added space and dignity, and there was a fair sprinkling of plush. Its location at Sixth and Commercial was central, and until destroyed by fire in 1892, it had vivid life.

Playbills of the day list very eminent artists: prima donna Emma Abbott in *Faust,* in November of '88, followed by Margaret Mather in *Romeo and Juliet;* the Standard Opera Company in *Iolanthe.* For actors, Otis Skinner, the popular Grismer-Davies Combination later. The early nineties enjoyed Maude Granger in *Inherited;* Cleveland's Consolidated Minstrels with Billy Emerson "the original, the only;" Emma Juch in *Carmen* and other operas. Frederick Warde, billed in *The Mountebank,* was held over a night at an $1,800 guarantee to play *Virginius.* There was a thriving local amateur group, and singer Miss Katie Flavel, trained by Marchesi, entertained townsmen in a benefit for the library. For the definitely less ethereal skidroaders, a movable platform set up on wooden horses made it possible to stage prize fights. John L. Sullivan fought here, later returning on stage in *The Village Blacksmith*. Here flourished such rough-hewn drama as *Jon Jonson,* in which was used the famous buzzsaw scene from *Blue Jeans*.

Along the coast in the last year of the eighties the Marshfield Odd Fellows, acutely conscious of civic need, built an aspiring structure with an opera house on its second floor. Used also for dances and political gatherings, it quickly edged out decrepit Norman's Hall as a community center. When a stage was built in, with wings and drop curtain thickly sprinkled with commercial ads, chairs replaced hard benches; flats and electric lights lured the players. Down from Portland by boat came the New Market troupe, presenting *Rosedale, or The Rifle Ball;* occasional touring companies from Frisco stopped in. Though later supplanted by the more modern Masonic Hall, this first opera house operated for many years, until burned in 1920. It also served North Bend and nearby towns.

The inland valley towns also lacked theatres. All through the eighties, Oregon City got along with its prim and solid Pope's Hall. And, throughout these widening circuits, practically the same travelling companies are found. The regional stock companies toured, in their repertory of tried favorites — the New Market troupe; later, John Cordray's players. Occasional road shows added an urban tone. Local players filled many a listless evening, and stray medicine shows enlivened the days.

Reed's Opera House at Salem had antedated the New Market by a full decade, but it sadly lacked the latter's velvet splendor and backstage aids. Large though it was, dressing rooms were bare and small, heating still achieved by noisy wood stoves. Curtain time was decided by the impatient audience, or by shrill whistles from the gallery gods. "Hawkins," inquired the able director of a prominent touring company of Reed's veteran caretaker, "what time do you ring up the curtain?" "Well, sir," was the answer, "when you hear the folks out there begin to stomp, I reckon it's time to begin." In the spacious nigger heaven, gamins had bored many auger holes, the better to see and hear what went on down below.

Regrettably down at heels by the eighties, Reed's was yet to round out a full thirty years of service. Practically all touring companies stopped there; fair week brought extended billings. Even the siren spell of the town's bars, the Last Chance, the Germania, the North Star, the Tontine, suffered at times from greater enchantment. Singers Emma Nevada and Ellen Yaw, actors Frederick Warde, Louis James, Robert Mantell, together with Fanny Rice, the Black Patti, Pudd'nhead Wilson and Sousa's famous band all appeared here during the eighties. Reed's closed in a blaze of glory and nostalgic memories, with Barlow's Minstrels, in April of 1900, just as the town's more modern Grand Theatre was nearing completion.

Little red plush cheered the smaller towns, despite the heady march of progress. Albany was too often by-passed. Though Corvallis had an opera house of sorts, built in the mid-seventies, as late as 1890, the *Gazette,* speaking editorially, deplored the lack of a proper theatre in the town. Listing sorely needed changes in heating, lighting and seating facilities, it adds: "It is time that something is done to this place for amusements, and with the change will come dramatic companies who have a first-class reputation, and not the snide shows that have been afflicting the people here for the past ten years. Of course, this house will be no Marquam Grand or Alcazar, but it will be good enough for anyone in these parts—providing, of course, the improvements are made." The changes were duly made, and throughout the nineties the town enjoyed a greatly improved dramatic climate. Even so, far too many bell ringers, oddities and minor shows lingered in the region.

Eugene, later a notable dramatic center, was not much better off with its ramshackle Rhinehart's Theatre. Its so-called boxes might surprise occupants by suddenly scooting them down to the floor. Up near the ceiling, colored Japanese lanterns swayed in its drafts. But, thanks to its convenient mid-valley location, most San Francisco companies en route to Portland stopped overnight here, and the eighties furnished solid fare. Billings included James A.

Herne in his own play, *Sag Harbor;* Clara Morris in *La Martyre;* Belleford and Brophy in *The Planter's Wife;* the Stutz Dramatic Company in repertory; Nellie Boyd and Charles Maubury in *Natural Life;* the Boston Opera Company; the Georgia Minstrels, amid a lengthy list. It was a dressy place; the ladies loved to turn out in full regalia for the more special events.

Down in southern Oregon, Jacksonville was deep in civic drama. Center of this was its famed United States Hotel, erected in 1880 on the ashes of the old Horn Hotel. Its hostess, French Madame Holt, earlier from New Orleans, made the town sit up and notice when she rode, stylishly dressed, behind her spanking bays along its cobbled streets. The new hotel had a built-in stage and dressing rooms, one duly marked with a star. The auditorium of Holt's Hall, as it was called, used also as a ballroom, became the scene of brilliant gatherings. Downstairs were several elegant suites, each with its own fireplace—all this in keeping with the grandeur of an inn that housed—and fleeced—a president. The retort of President Hayes, astonished at a bill of $240 for a night's lodging for himself and small staff, that he "hadn't intended to buy the place," is still cherished round about.

Holt's Hall throughout the eighties shared thespian honors with brewer Veit Schutz' Hall. It led off with a Grand Fourth of July Ball; the president came in September, 1880. Various touring companies were here billed: Vernelle's Company; John Malone in Shakespearean plays; Morell's Minstrels and others. The dashing steeds of the old California and Oregon stage line, thundering into town, left overtones never since lost.

But a neighboring village, only a dot on the map when the eighties began, soon stole the spotlight. Medford, five miles distant, platted in 1883, granted a railway franchise refused by the older town. Job seekers, both transients and stayers, drifted in, and belatedly, its stage annals take over in mid-decade. Its tiny Angle Opera House, lighted by gas, with a stage described by oldtimers as "the size of a row boat," drew avid patrons. Even lurid melodrama with such titles as *The Devil* could fill its hard seats. Soon, however, road shows from California, minstrels and concerts eked out the meagre fare.

The town grew fast, and it liked theatre. The touring shows, often with large casts, out of pocket in true player fashion, must book for box office to ensure their northward fare. By 1887 travelling companies were billing Medford instead of fading J'ville. The plays were better and more frequent; to house them the larger Wilson Opera House was built in the last years of the decade. This was a downstairs theatre, fairly well equipped as to stage and seating. Renamed the Medford Theatre, it functioned through the '90s, visited by touring celebrities. When destroyed by fire, it was replaced by the more modern Page Theatre, early in the new century.

Still farther south, Ashland rode to the fore with the railroads. Its tiny upstairs Houck's Hall cramped the swelling audiences; so too did Myers Hall and McCall's. But at least the touring companies were stopping: the Vernelle Troupe; Langrishe, the comedian. Late in the decade, its new and modern Gagniard Theatre, "one of the finest in the state," was built, opening with the nineties. Earlier, plays had occasionally been put on at the Stage House at nearby Phoenix, once called Gasburg.

The frontier lingered long in this southern mountain country. Far down in the '80s, the *Ashland Tidings,* listing various road shows, notes as well daring stage robberies by Black Bart or fellow bandits holed out in the rugged terrain between there and Grants Pass. There were many claims for bounty on gray wolves round about also.

In the sagebrush stretches beyond, red plush was definitely lacking. Even that hustling boom town, Baker City, was no exception. But Rust's wooden opera house, built in the '70s, was a major stop for players making the Salt Lake City-Idaho-Montana swing. Listed in the '80s are Nellie Boyd, Katie Putnam, Jo Jefferson in *Rip Van Winkle,* James O'Neill in *The Count of Monte Cristo,* Kate Claxton in *The Two Orphans.* Long before the trains arrived in '84, there were many fine plays. Southern companies headed for Boise and beyond might take the inland stage, or continue down river from The Dalles. Oldtimers relay tales of a passing burlesque show which plastered the landscape with garish posters of "girls in pink tights," to the horror of the town. But, they add with relish, "the show did well."

Pendleton's prosperous wheat and cattle farmers exchanged a dreary succession of halls for Fraser's Opera House in 1886. This sturdy two-story brick playhouse was not without worthy visitors, among them Barrie's *Little Minister*. It was here that Frederick Warde was approved by Umatilla braves in *Virginius*. A current double *Uncle Tom's Cabin* troupe stopped by. In this two Little Evas, one wearing a pink and one a blue ribbon, divided honors in the same role during the evening.

The frontier lingered beyond the wide Columbia as well. In neighboring Washington, Spokane was still beset with sagebrush. In his memoirs, *Fifty Years of Make Believe*, Frederick Warde mentions playing in this theatre-loving town in 1885 "over a fire-house" to a "remarkably cultivated and appreciative audience." For an appearance of Emma Abbott, with a $10,000 guarantee, legend smilingly reports seats sold on farm tractors, stored in the town's only sizable hall. Its slapdash Gaiety Theatre was a favorite haunt of roving troupers. So too at Walla Walla, where players paused, going or coming, at its stand-by Variety Theatre. Olympia, the state's capital, had long loved the mummers, but, off-center for the railroads, it did not build its handsome Olympic Theatre until the nineties.

Main challenge to the New Market's red plush came from brisk Seattle, where in 1884 Frye's fine opera house was built on downtown First Avenue. Patterned by its architect, John Nestor, after San Francisco's Baldwin Theatre, it was at once heralded by the press as "the largest theatre north of that place." Lavish indeed were its decorations of "brown plush with a band of red plush at the top," draperies in red and gold, a very heavy green velvet carpet with large red roses, and a magnificent chandelier turned on a short time before curtain." In "comfort, acoustic, stage accommodations and safety," states the Seattle directory of '85, Frye's Opera House ranks with any on the coast. Its ample stage, thirty-six by forty feet, its dressing rooms and green room, latest fire equipment, proscenium and fashion boxes, comfortable opera chairs and other splendors are fully listed. The four-story brick and iron structure, costing $100,000, contained stores and offices. Lighted by gas, the opera house was likewise equipped with a movable hardwood floor for dancing.

Frye's, replacing the town's "first real theatre"—Squire's Opera House, built five years before—opened with eclat. Nellie Boyd with leading man Theodore Roberts on December 1, 1884, presented *Forget Me Not* and *To Oblige Benson*. It was a brilliant social event; on the second night, fringed satin programs signed by the star were distributed. There followed a long succession of stellar attractions: Mr. and Mrs. McKee-Rankin in Joaquin Miller's *Forty Nine* and *The Danites;* the Baldwin Theatre Company in *Shadows of a Great City,* with young Maude Adams in the cast; William Gillette and the Madison Square Players in *The Private Detective* and *The Rajah;* Grace Hawthorne in *Camille;* Lewis Morrison in Belasco's *May Blossom.* The Thompson Opera Company played in January of 1886 to "the largest and most fashionable audience ever assembled at the Opera House;" Bill Nye lectured to "a much larger house than his exercises merited."

On the road in 1887 were Emma Abbott's Grand English Opera Company of fifty-five members and a twelve-piece orchestra; George Milne in *Richelieu, Hamlet* and *Macbeth;* Cort's Standard Theatre Company in vaudeville. Annie Pixley, "long a favorite with Seattle audiences," drew glowing notices in *The Deacon's Daughter* and *Charity Girl,* "her Washtub song and others repeatedly encored." Polar Bear Sam's Alaskan Indians (eight braves and as many squaws) performed in native dances and songs. But tragic Madame Janauschek also "held the house enthralled" in the death scene of the old Gypsy Queen in *Meg Merrilies.* Solid dramatic fare, well laced with variety.

A shouting match immediately ensued between the Northwest's two largest cities as to the size and grandeur of their respective opera houses. Manager Beede had proudly advertised Frye's as "the largest and most complete north of Portland;" the press would settle for nothing less than "the largest north of San Francisco." Manager Howe of the New Market, in a full page ad in San Francisco's authoritative *Music and Drama,* placed his theatre as "the largest, handsomest and most complete west of St. Paul by the N. P. RR, and north of San Francisco . . ." Well, that was that!

The opera bouffe battle blazed for months. Census figures of the towns crept in (Portland just then ahead); test audience counts for Georgie Woodthorpe's week's run, with sly hints that noted stars would not pause for "one or two nights billing en route." One haughty letter contended that neither playhouse could hold a candle to Victoria's splendid Royal Theatre, opened in January of '86, and "fitted in most elegant manner at a cost of $70,000." It had fourteen full sets of scenery! . . . But perhaps all the loud shouting merely meant that the raw-boned Northwest had finally settled down to full enjoyment of its well-loved stage. And so it certainly had.

But shrewd Manager Howe held the aces. As booking manager for the entire region, his ad for the New Market on March 7, 1885, covered all northern circuit towns: "Olympia, New Tecoma [sic], Seattle, Pt. Townsend, Victoria and New Westminster, B. C." It ended on this devastating note: "I can date companies from two to four weeks in the above theatres and on circuit. Managers and agents contemplating a tour of the Northwest will find it to their advantage to address me at once." Listing companies already booked, Howe adds as a final barb: "Portland, Oregon, population 40,000, acknowledged to be the best paying city of its size for all attractions of established reputation."

Population as well as theatre ratings were to vary somewhat in later days, but to the troupers all the furore merely assured them of two handsome theatres to play in, instead of yesterday's bare halls. The golden days of the road show and of resident stock were yet to come. And a spectre haunted the eighties: the touring "combination," a make-shift playing group.

The oldtime combination, as elsewhere noted, was too often rounded up for the far western tour from shabby New York rooming houses, smothering some big-name player in cheaper "ham" actors. Many fine ensembles such as the Madison Square Players were on tour, but far too many third-rate ones. The columns of *Music and Drama,* current arbiter of the fine arts, crackled with indignation at the whole combination system, which unloaded its dramatic 'has beens' on the luckless West. As seen, much impressive theatre was abroad, but the shoddy combinations were to prove later dynamite.

A brief Howe-Beede merger, in the late '80s, ended the inter-city feud. Frye's became Seattle's "Only Combination House;" Manager Howe, for the New Market retained only the adjective "handsome." The beautiful lady had just received a face-lifting, in deference to younger rivals, when suddenly—tragedy! In Seattle, the cruel holocaust of July, 1889 burned out the town's business district, and with it Frye's Opera House. One of its last players was Effie Essler in *Hazel Kirke,* the name role she had created in the East, bringing praise from critics for her freedom from the current "ranting and violent action." Strangely, she had also given the final performance at the town's first opera house — Squire's — before it was remade into the Brunswick Hotel in 1883.

As for the New Market, her reign had already been challenged — and in her own town — by a brash rival. The city was moving back from the riverfront to higher ground. Business blocks were rising out where cow pastures had been. In November of '84, the much less splendid Casino opened at Washington and Park, starring Jeanie Winston in a swinging musical, *Donna Juanita.* Small cafe tables, in the manner of San Francisco's popular resorts, invaded the floor. At lower prices — seventy-five, fifty, twenty-five cents — songbird Jeanie nightly charmed full houses in *Boccacio, Fra Diavolo* and other light operas. Singers Bessie King, Louise Lester and a succession of engaging sirens followed. During the summer, such able combinations as the Wallack Company in *Lady Clair* carried on. The stately New Market, remodelled early in 1884, drew loyal fans to the end. But the play, *Shadows of a Great City,* given in the fall of 1887 by the excellent Alcazar Company with a carload of scenery, was perhaps prophetic. Its final offering, Milton Nobles in his own play, *Phoenix,* held more distant promise.

In one of the endless deals of show business, Manager Howe shortly moved out to the Casino. The famous red plush benches went with him. When urbane Mr. Howe removed to New York for a time, John Cordray assumed its management. Reluctantly, in a later remodelling, the upholstered benches, symbol of a passing splendor, were broken up by stage director Louis Fried. The aging New Market, now a warehouse, could not protest . . . But by then the lush nineties had waltzed into the scene. The coast cities were playing a game called Top This! which called for even greater magnificence, in the theatre as elsewhere.

And by then the entire Northwest scene had shifted, and with it the smaller backdrop. The off-stage noises were different, too; the rising hum of the machine had drowned out the woodman's axe; the deep-throated voices of the city had long silenced the lonely cry of the coyote.

In a quiet by-street, a deposed queen dreamed of breathless days, of magic nights, to the splash of a nearby fountain, with restless pigeons criss-crossing the red sun . . . Progress was busy with her latest plaything: a new century.

THEATRE OLIO

The rich exuberance of the theatre has never lent itself to neat packaging. Lines suddenly fade out; the accepted types freely borrow from each other. The oldtime trouper, one minute spouting Shakespeare from extempore platforms, the next indulging in outrageous farce, did little for the unities. And the hard-living frontier, like young America in general, had scant time for fine distinctions. Good entertainment, lively and diverse, would do nicely, thank you.

Now, facing sophistication, the stage embraced a motley crew. Most of these were akin to the Legitimate, though not all in the genteel tradition. Certain earthy relatives now press for attention, edging out early gypsy hangers-on—the wagon shows, the big top—already noted. Mainly dedicated to mirth, they were tonic in times of stress. Some, like the settlers, had followed the course of empire westward. One or two were to share their changing fortunes.

THE BLACKFACE BOYS

The South had bred the minstrel tradition. There, as far back as 1829, solo recreations of negro plantation ballads and lively Jim Crow dances had been current. The vogue spread to New England, following an appearance in Boston of the Virginia Serenaders in 1840. This was a quartette organized by Dan Emmett, later a famed exponent of Ethiopian roles. It quickly swept New York, then outward and westward, gaining fresh force as fresh acts and music were added. Its tuneful ditties were hummed everywhere: "Blue-Tailed Fly" or "Such a Gittin' Upstairs." Many of Stephen Foster's finest ballads, still cherished today, were written for minstrel production.

The minstrel show's folksy delineation of negro character, its rousing banjo rhythms and nostalgic ballads struck a common chord. Such eminent writers as Bayard Taylor and visiting William M. Thackeray found its unpretentious folk airs moving, its colorful vignettes of lowly plantation life refreshing after the heavy melodrama far too often on stage. It bequeathed to the American stage one of its most original and native traditions.

It was notably easy. Burnt cork was to be had for the reaching; banjos were plentiful. In the wake of the gold rush of '49, minstrel shows swept the West Coast; even en route, on shipboard, rounding the Horn, its lively rhythms had alternated with social dancing. A minstrel show had led off in California's dramatic roster, put on by soldiers of Captain Stevenson's New York Volunteers, along with melodrama and farces, in the mid-forties. In the high Sierras, miners loved its swift movement and melody; the fifties swayed with its rhythms.

In the Northwest, the dog-trot cabins were scarcely roofed than Bones and Sambo got under way. It was the settlers, here, who took to burnt cork to outwit monotony. The workaday life of frontier Oregon had its full quota of gay moments, judging from a spectator's notes of that day.

"The first minstrel troupe to come before an audience in the Northwest," declares the Native Son of December, 1900, "was composed of pioneers . . . from Oregon City. They were Mr. Wm. Chance, bones; John Bartlett, violin; Dr. W. McCracken, triangle; Mr. Carlyle, trombone. Their initial performance was given in Portland on December 2, 1850, at the residence of Simeon G. Reed, whose dining room had been turned into a temporary theatre. Mr. Reed was paid $50 for the use of his residence for two hours. He was also required to furnish the tallow candles used to light the same during the performance. Everybody paid $1 admission, and the house was full. The troupe came down from Oregon City by steamer, but in order to save expense, walked back to that place. On reaching Milwaukie on the return trip, they found a mill there on fire. All water on hand being frozen, they fought the flames with snowballs, and with them succeeded in quenching the fire. The other towns visited were Oregon City, Butteville, Champoeg and Salem. The season being ended, they found their profit amounted to seventy-five cents. They however had "oceans of fun."

Professional minstrels reached the Northwest on the heels of the circus, mainly from the south by way of the Sierra mining camps. The San Francisco Minstrels shook the rafters of the upstairs Portland Theatre in April of '58; the Excelsior Minstrels, listed in July of the same year, featured famous Dan Watson as "Old Eph." During October the *Oregon Weekly Times* notes the presence in Portland of the Taylor Brothers Minstrels "in connection with the best performers on the coast, and among whom we notice America's own jig dancer, Mike Mitchell," famed exponent of the Rattlesnake Plantation Jig. It adds: "All those troubled with 'down in the mouf' had better spend an evening with the minstrel boys." In November, the minstrels are editorially commended along with the Chapman Family and "Balls, routs and other attractions that lately have made our town quite gay." Certainly the struggling village could use some laughter.

Travelling light, the early minstrels could perform on almost any stage. Oregon and California knew no cultural barriers; Washington was a bare step farther. All along the West Coast, minstrels are numerous in the sixties; they are rampant in the seventies. It was in the eighties, however, that they took on grandeur, as did all else in the theatre. Major companies such as George Christy's or Primrose and West travelled in state with forty (count 'em) members, in private cars. Carrying their own orchestra, scenery and eye-blinding costumes, they played the largest theatres: the Marquam Grand, Reed's, the plush Seattle. Street parades boomed out their arrival, and with famed national figures as end men, they could be counted on for sell-out crowds anywhere. The small towns dearly loved wise-cracking Bones and Sambo; the soft shoe dancers, the lively ballads. Main Streets would be lined as high-stepping performers strutted by in tall hats and outrageous costumes, a noisy band shattering the silence of the soft firs.

Far too numerous for listing, the names show an infinite variety: the Black Baby Boy Minstrels, the Fairy Minstrels (a child ensemble), the "Refined" Minstrels, among a host of others. The Male and Female Minstrels from San Francisco's Metropolitan Theatre, featuring "The Inimitable Lotta," have already been noted on their Northwest tour. The Diamond Minstrels, "late of New York," played the Willamette soon after. The Oro Fino lists the Apollo Minstrels on September 28, 1866; the Tanner Troupe of Ethiopian Minstrels the next year. At the same theatre occurred a mammoth Benefit for Dan Watson, "one of the first negro minstrels who ever visited Oregon." Headlined was a highly rated monolog by "Old Eph."

The more plethoric olio of such glittering aggregations as Christy's might include flutists, contortionists, and various variety numbers. A Grand Opening Number would be followed by solo performances of featured players, rising to a crashing Ensemble by the whole company. For the Afterpiece—usually dramatic—burlesques and extravaganzas were popular. Take-offs on the more serious offerings of the stage, with Shakespeare and opera as favorite targets, flaunted such titles as *Medea, or The Best of Mothers; Romeo and Juliet, or The Cup of Cold Pizen; Hotel d'Afrique, or The Mistakes of a Night.*

Blackface took on new bounce and vigor in the '80s when jazz surged into the scene. Strutting cakewalks, with ragtime and rocking syncopated rhythms later animated the nineties — precursors of today's blues, bop, bebop and primitive rhythms in general. The decline of blackface confirmed a change in the life of the negro, a basic change in the American scene, and for that matter, in the American theatre. Many of its acts were absorbed by vaudeville.

THE MUSEE'-THEATRES

One of the more bizarre unions between the serious legitimate stage and a lower-browed scion produced that strange dramatic hybrid known as the musee'-theatre. Imported into the Northwest by tycoon John F. Cordray, they were already popular in the Midwest and farther east. Not only did they provide a standard stage and theatre, offering current favorites done by reputable stock companies, but a downstairs museum as well. The latter, set forth with a good-sized variety stage, added numerous sideshows and animal acts. Catching the settler coming and going, the double-barrelled appeal was potent. This was intensified by an early evening concert.

Cordray, arriving young and hopeful in Portland in the late eighties, already had behind him fifteen years of experience in managing combined museums and theatres in New York, Chicago, St. Louis and New Orleans. He soon exchanged a transient "store show" down on the riverfront for a more permanent stand farther uptown at Third and Yamhill. Here, on the site of a former lumber yard, "occupying a quarter of a block, surrounded by a ramshackle fence, and bordered by a few scraggly shade trees," he erected a huge tented structure. It was soon transformed into his Musee'-Theatre, a "place of amusement comparable in comfort, completeness and quality with any in the United States, except for a few leading grand opera houses, and possessing some appointments not to be found in these."

Its walls combined a roomy upstairs theatre with modern stage, where "actors of ability" faced the footlights, with the smaller downstairs stage presenting "variety entertainments of high order," plus the various sideshows mentioned. Cordray's Musee'-Theatre opened July 1, 1889, headlining in its theatre proper the Essie Tittell Dramatic Company, organized expressly for this purpose, in the popular play *Lynwood, or The Rifle Ball*. A dazzling collection of variety acts enlivened the downstairs stage, added to the large assemblage of Musee' attractions. Crowds flocked to the new place of entertainment, often straining its seating capacity of 1,500.

By some unknown feat of magic, the big tent was gradually converted into a "solid two-story structure roofed with corrugated iron and having an ornamental tower and bandstand on the corner," without a performance being missed. For a half hour before curtain time, a sixteen-piece band discoursed classical and popular music from the tower. And there was plenty of plush in the theatre proper—all upholstery done in a brilliant peacock blue. This graced the patent folding opera chairs, the railings and box partitions, even the gallery. Only in the ten-cent section were chairs retained. The ample stage was equipped throughout with "incandescent electric lights," as was the auditorium; and, very early, with a brand-new gadget, a dimmer. Prices, however, were popular, ranging from ten to sixty cents; thirty cents for orchestra chairs, the top price being for boxes.

During its several years of operation, the Musee's stock company, aided by its own orchestra, produced most of the better current plays. The starring Tittell Sisters, Essie and Minnie, were prime favorites in the Northwest. Supported by R. E. French and other stalwarts, they toured at intervals, often exchanging with Cordray's later Seattle troupe. In all the Cordray theatres, the family atmosphere was strongly emphasized. Liquor was strictly forbidden, and special police were on hand to enforce decorum. Rules printed on playbills forbade "catcalls, and boisterous behavior," even the eating of peanuts. Cordray remained to the end a stickler for clean offerings on stage and in the lives of his actors.

In the downstairs Musee', an hour's variety show featured rising singers, dancers or impersonators. Many a later star of the entertainment world got his start on some such minor stage; throughout the nineties, the two-a-days spun brightly. Gymnasts, acrobats and trained animal acts were also popular.

Entrance to the Musee' was directly from the street—admission, one thin dime. This sufficed for both the variety program and the sideshows. Here numerous strange objects, alive or mechanical, at once engaged the spectator's attention. Chief among them was a huge electric clock of Cordray's own invention. This contained more than 100 moving figures, including the twelve apostles, the various heavenly bodies and others. It also "gave instructive illustrations in Astronomy, and played an array of Musical selections." Farther on, one might encounter women glass blowers in action, knife throwers, Egyptian mummies, snake charmers or other thrillers. A circus of thirty trained dogs drew in crowds; a Punch and Judy show enthralled the children. Patrons often lingered before the square glass peep-hole of a cosmorama—distant forbear of the modern movie.

The dime museum was at the moment a national institution. Caged animals of exotic origin, alligators, boa constrictors, even "blood-sucking vampires" chilled the spine; captive birds and the usual unhappy crew of lions, tigers, or monkeys added a vocal protest. It all appealed to the love of novelty, of the strange, the bizarre—and, possibly, to the imagination. Certainly there was an assault on the senses. The vogue of the dime museum continued in many parts of the country until well down in the nineties.

Eminently successful, for his Seattle Musee'-Theatre Cordray soon after remodelled the aging Madison Street Theatre at Third Avenue, formerly a Toklas-Singerman store building. Here the same two-stage plan was followed; the familiar tower built on, and the theatre proper handsomely upholstered, again in blue plush. Folding opera seats, carpets, steam heat and 500 lights were installed; its stage, thirty feet deep and eighty wide, was fitted to "present any opera or spectacular play." A New York artist, employed for scene design, produced a drop curtain of Moorish background. A built-in horseshoe balcony brought the seating capacity to 1,400 persons.

The grand entrance to the downstairs Musee', under the corner tower, blazed with arc lights; its smaller auditorium seated only 100 persons. But, for the same dime admission, these might witness "the Cream of the Specialties"—an hour of vaudeville which preceded the regular stage play given upstairs. For this, the tariff was twenty, thirty, forty cents, with boxes for half a dollar. An estimated $20,000 was spent in the remodelling, and here the animal show was muted.

Cordray's Seattle Musee' opened on December 1, 1890, with *The Lady of Lyons*. Seats were auctioned to prevent favoritism, and three years of almost constant operation followed. As the largest playhouse in town, it was rented by John Hanna for Bernhardt in *Fedora* on September 21, 1891. When the new and much more splendid Seattle Theatre was built in 1892, Cordray, in competition, engaged the entire company from San Francisco's Alcazar for that season, to replace his regular resident stock company. Here too the same emphasis on family theatre prevailed, with strict rules of behavior. Rechristened the Third Avenue, after later remodelling, under changing management it did yeoman service in the town's life until the early years of the present century. Mainly this was through the efforts of a series of excellent stock companies there resident.

Cordray's Portland Musee', by strange chance also located on a Third Avenue, likewise supported a durable stock company. Members of the original Tittell Dramatic ensemble, with R. E. French as lead, gravitated between the two towns, before giving ways to newer troupes. Various national stars also faced its footlights, but the Portland Cordray's gained most solid fame as the first home of the popular Baker Stock Company. With the menagerie long banished, and under changing names, it did faithful service until condemned in 1910.

THE CHINESE THEATRE

The region had its own olio — but of people. Some record of alien theatre within the new frontier is here timely. Caught in the westward-running tide, French-Canadians, Irish, Swedes, Finns elbowed Yankees and Southerners, all driven by much the same urges. But the Caucasians, in general, sat down together in whatever crude opera house presented itself. They applauded the same actors, and in the end became much the same composite American. It remained for Chinese emigrants—and there were many of these—to transport their own theatre to the new frontier, in all its strange and topsy-turvy splendor.

It was during the years of most intensive building—from the '60s through the '80s—that the greatest influx of Orientals to the West Coast of America took place. The discovery of gold had triggered the movement; soon every mining town had its quota of blue-bloused Chinese, patient and unvocal except in their own tongue, and too often targets for frontier horseplay. Not only did they figure hugely in the labor picture of that day, but they made good copy for its writers. Bret Harte used them freely; so too did Joaquin Miller in his rough-hewn dramas.

As the restless placer miners moved on to supposedly richer quartz diggings, the slower Chinese somehow managed to make day's wages in their wake. The trail led upward through the Siskiyous, along the Rogue River through Jacksonville; farther north by way of Scottsburg and the John Day country; into Idaho, Montana and the farthest corners of the region.

Nor was that all. The heavy task of "letting daylight into the swamp," as the lumbermen define progress, created labor shortages everywhere. New-built mills and canneries, new-plowed farms, new-founded hotels drew heavily on Oriental industry. Trade expanded; as early as 1866, regional financier Ben Holladay had purchased the steamer *Oriflamme* for trade with China. The establishment of a military shipping point at Port Orford and the placing of the steamer *Columbia* on the coast run were added factors in pulling Chinese immigration northward.

Mainly the incoming stream flowed through the Golden Gate, and scores of confused strangers settled within the comforting shadows of San Francisco's Chinatown, with its familiar joss-houses and burrowing alleys. But the northern ports, Portland, Seattle, Victoria and Vancouver, gave more direct access to mines and canneries of the Northwest and British Columbia. Mass labor contracts were negotiated by merchants or head men located in these key cities, but smaller details of passage were looked after by the powerful "Six Companies," so-called because they represented various provinces from which the labor was recruited. Much of this was Cantonese. These companies, forerunners of the modern Chinese Benevolent Society, also furnished interpreters en route, met the bewildered stranger on landing, and took care that he was absorbed by the proper tong in the new land. Records of the six companies show that between 1850 and 1869 they had brought into this country 135,586 persons, many later returned or buried, according to contract. And this was comparatively low tide.

Later, during the dramatic race of the railroads across the continent, owners of the Union Pacific and Central Pacific—Huntington, Stanford, Mark Hopkins—imported 10,000 Chinese coolies to push the roadbeds through the deserts and across the mountains. Results are part of our national story. Oregon's railways, likewise: the Oregon Central, the Oregon Pacific, the O.W.R. & N. — and others in Washington and British Columbia — were constructed largely by Chinese labor. So too were many other Northwest projects. By 1885, the period when anti-Chinese agitation began boiling up from the sand-lots of California, many thousands of Chinese were settled on the West Coast, though with small likelihood that the Pacific Coast, as hinted by fanatics, was in danger of becoming a distant province of China.

With labor shortages eased, lean years brought ugly anti-Chinese riots throughout the three coast states during depressed days of the late '80s. Grim vendettas between rival tongs played out their dark dramas as late as the 1920s, in urban back alleys. Most small towns had their Chinese laundry, but it was the cities that offered fruitful audiences for a separate Chinese theatre.

Portland alone, for example, during the winters of '85 and '86, just before the agitation mentioned, was home for an estimated 12,000 Orientals. In addition to seasonal workers on railroads, canneries or mills, many served as freighters, laundrymen or barbers. Still others functioned notably as domestics, with a devotion still remembered by first families round about.

Portland's bulging Chinatown sprawled through several blocks down near the river on Second Avenue, from Oak to Yamhill and beyond. Exotic bazaars, assorted shops, fish markets, laundries and eating places crowded this strip, and some of the town's most flourishing mercantile firms were located here, paying very fancy rents to keep their foothold. Chinese shops were then provided with wooden awnings to keep off rain, and old newspapers of the '80s contain vivid sketches of this populous thoroughfare. Night or day, throngs of chattering Celestials—then so called—might be encountered, bartering, visiting, or smoking pipes "big as a thimble," with stems three feet long. Portland's Chinese colony included persons of culture: officials, merchants and such. To all its patrons the theatre—three of them at different times—offered a replica of playhouses which were so much a part of daily life in the distant homeland.

The main or 'old' Chinese theatre, still vividly remembered by pioneers, ran for more than twenty years; roughly from about 1879 to 1904. It was located in the midst of the Chinese quarter at Second and Alder. The large upstairs room in which plays were given was reached by a stairway from populous Second Avenue. Approximately 100 feet square, its center was furnished with wooden benches, as in China; a number of crude boxes or wooden stalls circled the room, each large enough for several people. The stage, twenty-five feet in depth, ran long the back wall. Outside were living rooms for the actors. These were professionals, prepared by years of training. The highly patterned Chinese stage did not lend itself to the amateur.

The orchestra, so essential to Chinese theatre, sat along the rear of the stage, smoking or chatting informally when not playing —which was seldom indeed. The Chinese play is basically a music-drama, with most of its dialogue sung as in opera. There is musical accompaniment throughout from flutes or a two-stringed violin weaving the lighter passages. Heavier effects—battles or duels—are accented by brass, percussion, and the beating of drums or tom-toms. There is lavish use of pantomime, highly symbolic in nature, to underline action. Indeed, the action at times is solely carried by such movement. Its meaning, traditional for centuries, is well known to the audience.

The stage, a raised platform about five feet high, was without front curtain, wings or footlights. A brilliant hanging traditionally adorns the back wall, in which there are two doors — one for entrance, the other for exit. Some movable props—mainly tables or chairs, with a few painted banners representing waves, clouds, perhaps a city wall—took care of settings. For the Chinese theatre does not depend on realism for its effects. Instead, as in Shakespeare's day, it draws upon the imagination of its audience. At a word, a sign, walled cities, heaving battlefields, a palace, a hovel appear. One symbolic gesture may be the climax of tragedy—a defeated prince, a dying warrior. The magic carpet does the rest.

Spectators in the Second Avenue theatre — mostly male — sat about on the stiff wooden benches, munching dried watermelon seeds or li-chee nuts in most approved fashion. In old China, theatre benches were provided with a convenient shelf along the back, for lunch items or teapots. The habitue' took his theatre seriously, and planned to stay awhile—as well he might. Five hour sessions were not unusual; in all coast towns a clock, visible to the audience, was standard equipment. The plays began at seven o'clock or earlier; if they ended before midnight, patrons could ask for their money back. Since there were no intermissions, the audience drifted in or out, sipping tea or smoking. Meanwhile on stage the actors, in gorgeous peacock costumes, fought their mimic battles or galloped about on horseback (in pantomime) with complete concentration and skill. Hawkers of cakes, nuts or fruit pressed their wares; in the older country steaming towels wrung from hot water were flung about at intervals so that patrons might wipe face, neck or hands as needed. They paid close attention to the plays when seated. These followed the colorful tradition of the ancient Chinese stage based on past history.

The plays were not, as with us, divided into tragedy or comedy, but into military (wu) and civil (wen) offerings. Since most of them fell into the first category, battles were as numerous as fist fights in a modern Western. But with exactly opposite usage. Should an unlucky actor, in the furious lungings and wheelings required in Chinese stage battles (often with four-foot swords) directly touch an opponent, he would brand himself—but literally so—a bad actor. Fit subject for cat-calls, if there were any such. But the Chinese audience seldom applauded or showed emotion of any sort. The impassive dead-pan, however, masked a deep love of theatre and its mimic play.

The Portland theatres were usually crowded. One touring company, the N'Gun-Sho-Lin troupe from San Francisco, remained several weeks, offering a complete cycle of plays, brilliantly costumed. Admission was a thrifty thirty-five cents, collected at the head of the stairs. Special police protection was then afforded the district, because of crowded conditions. Floors were kept clean, no matter how dingy the stairway, and the inevitable teapot was not lacking. Programs of plays posted downstairs in the street drew attentive crowds. Oldtimers have vivid memories of Portland's bulging Chinatown, and of steamers chugging up-river, filled with emigrants in bamboo hats and long queues.

Though the audience of the Second Avenue Theatre was mainly Chinese, occasional uptown visitors drifted in. Its stiff benches were topped by the traditional wooden railing, four or five inches wide, and patrons would now and then perch on these, letting their feet rest on the bench below. Shoes might be slipped off, for tired feet, and this custom of rail sitting was at times highly practical. Tong wars were just then at their height along the entire West Coast. At any sign of trouble, the audience, thus poised, could quickly slip under the benches or out of doors as needed. At times the need was real. The old theatre, normally quiet and inoffensive, was the scene of an off-stage killing by a "soft blow" (hatchet) during one such vendetta.

Such happenings in and around the old Chinese theatre in its later years did not increase its uptown patronage. Passage of Exclusion Acts about this time cut down its Oriental audience. The fabulous bazaars, too, were edging away from the waterfront, as was the town itself. By 1904 its checkered career had ended;

it was remodelled into a cafe. But the town's legitimate theatres were also on the move—and away from the river.

At its height, Portland's Chinatown had needed more than one theatre. A smaller playhouse, opened in 1882 at Second and Yamhill, ran for several years. Actors from this and other theatres often danced the Dragon Dance in the street for Chinese New Year, weddings or other festivals. To serve overflow crowds, a third theatre, much more elaborately equipped, was later opened at Second and Oak streets. Here, in true Chinese fashion, a changing repertory of plays was given. A company of child actors from San Francisco played several weeks, as did other excellent troupes. When finally dismantled, its lush furnishings were auctioned. One of these, a handsomely carved mural panel representing in black and gold scenes from Chinese theatre, now enriches the foyer of Portland's Civic Theatre. The travelling companies made a wide arc, direct from China, with stops at major cities of the nation.

Cosmopolitan Seattle had a large Oriental population and teeming Chinatown, down toward Yesler Way. The first Chinese company to play in Washington Territory—the Von Soo Fong Troupe of eight members—led off at Yesler's old wooden Pavilion at Front and Cherry as early as 1876, as recorded by Grant in his *Story of Early Seattle Theatres*. Many companies followed, and a regular Chinese theatre operated at Second and Alder between 1883 and 1885 snuggled among joss-houses and devious alleys. Later, in 1892, the Chou Shi or Wong Lung Company of twenty-one first class artists, direct from China, with complete orchestra and costumes costing $10,000, performed at the Seattle Theatre. Tong wars long smoldered here in the restless Gateway City.

At Astoria also, site of some of the Northwest's largest canneries, there were many Chinese and a theatre of sorts. Later, aging Liberty Hall was for a time used as a Chinese theatre. This was around 1896 to 1898, according to Mrs. Polly McKean Bell, who adds: "A typical Oriental balcony was installed across the front, covered with Chinese characters in gold." Here, before each evening's performance, Chinese musicians would play their native instruments, thus attracting "many who were entertained by the high shrill notes of the Chinese fiddle, the clash of brass cymbals

and a high thin falsetto voice in some wailing Oriental melody."
It became popular among the young society group of the town
to visit the theatre, though an hour or two might satisfy their
curiosity. Major West Coast sites of year-round Chinese theatre
were San Francisco, Victoria and Vancouver, B. C.

VARIETY AND VAUDEVILLE

Vaudeville's expansive olio needs its own story. Something of
its swift surge into the Northwestern scene will appear in later
tales of its most ardent devotees; certain sidelights on its earlier
favor there have already been given. It has its own special hall of
fame—a host of players flashing like swallows across a summer
sky to leave their gift of laughter. In general, their contribution
was to a region, to a prevailing spirit—and for the moment.

Variety, as the settlers knew it, edged westward with the music
hall. Boston's venerable Howard Theatre has a highly colorful
past; so too has New York's Tony Pastor's. Both trained many
an unknown for the later Legitimate. Its shifting patterns cultivated ease and stage aplomb, most useful to the actor. As for
the audience, its flashing olio demanded little concentration for
enjoyment. The instructive was, in general, by-passed.

In the wake of California's gold rush, variety quickly invaded
San Francisco's blowsy music halls. A few pushed up under the
tall trees to follow the same pattern. Portland had its quota down
by the riverfront: the Tivoli, the Bijou, the Germania. Some had
small stages; on others, the floor show flourished. So likewise with
Seattle and Spokane. For the southern noisy melodeon the North
had its own counterpart: the skid road's brash store shows and
box houses of the Alaskan gold rush. Many a nondescript camp
had its own Bella Union or Bijou, where plentiful "red eye" made
laughter highly charged.

John Cordray's Musee'-Theatre, which also featured variety,
was, as noted, entirely different in temper. His insistence on clean
entertainment and swift rebuffs to roughness on stage or off, gave
troupers range and assurance for their artistry. And it was, at
times, definitely that. Farther north, Seattle's John Cort spent
money freely in his efforts to import high class entertainers even
before he moved permanently into the Legitimate field. The

gradual transformation of variety, mainly during the nineties, into the much more inclusive vaudeville, polite or otherwise, may be gleaned from the saga of its western champions, Considine and Pantages.

It is claimed* that in times of violent change and uncertainty, variety and spectacle dominate the stage. If so, the frontier's restless mood was well in tune with variety's swift changes. As for violence, the West Coast's stormy adolescence had plenty of that. In his entertaining study, *A History of Variety-Vaudeville in Seattle*, E. C. Elliott states: "Variety-Vaudeville received two great impetuses from the West that originated in comparable social conditions and gave variety bursts of life that were felt all the way to the Atlantic coast." These were the California gold rush and the later one to Alaska.

It may be noted in passing that it was in the Puget Sound country—Seattle, most notably—that variety took on Paul Bunyan proportions. And Seattle, as the above writer remarks, was not "a gentle city." Nor, for that matter was the Northwest gentle, either in geography or spirit. In its raw youth, particularly, there was little time for reflection. It was not wholly by chance that two of the Northwest's most canny showmen called Seattle home. Vaudeville's strong resurgence from there was wholly logical.

In its palmiest days, vaudeville drew to its footlights many top-flight entertainers: Mammy-singing Al Jolson, song-and-dance man George M. Cohan, lively Sophie Tucker, Eva Tanguay, the "I Don't Care Girl," and many another. It lured from the Legitimate, before it faded, such luminaries as the aging Bernhardt, famed prima donnas, noted actors. Its easy patterns were kind to clever people on the way up. Its timely gift of laughter was both pleasing and potent. It took a new century — and the threatening machine — to still its gay numbers.

At times, though, its flashing rhythms seemed a trifle empty; its patter somewhat hollow and forced. At moments man, the thinker, sought for whys and wherefores—in the wake of wars, notably, under pressure of pain and disillusion. And where, in all

*E. C. Elliott, *History of Variety-Vaudeville in Seattle from the Beginning to 1914* (University of Washington Press, 1944) , 6.

this groping world, did human passion so starkly unroll itself, in all its aspects, as on the stage—the legitimate stage, which grants, with full compassion, both laughter and tears?

For this, the thin trickle of touring road shows was plainly inadequate. For year-round theatre there was but one answer: the resident stock company.

The Oro Fino Theatre, on S.W. First three doors from Stark, was the setting for grand opera's Portland debut in 1867. The building was destroyed by fire in 1878. (*Oregonian* photo.)

Portland's Willamette Theatre was built in 1859, at First and Stark. Here the versatile playhouse doubles as an armory for the funeral of General E. R. S. Canby, killed by the Modoc Indians in 1873. (OHS Collections.)

Lotta Crabtree (top left), toast of the mining camps, first came into southern Oregon on a touring wagon in 1862. Lissome Jeanie Winston (left center) appeared in "Prince Methuselah" at the Casino, while Minnie Tittell (below left) was a great favorite on the Willamette Valley circuit. At right is Minnie Pixley, who with her sister Annie first appeared at Seattle's Yesler Hall in 1861, a theatre which had been the Yesler Mill cookhouse in 1852.

Stephen Masset (above), globe-trotting Thespian, toured Oregon in 1854. (Calif. So. of Pioneers.) John P. Howe (top left) was an early and successful theatrical manager in Seattle. (Courtesy of Elizabeth Benedict.) At left is builder of the New Market and patron of the theatre Alexander Ankeny. (OHS Collections.)

(Below) Copy of (George L.) Baker's Players weekly theatrical bulletin, 15,000 circulation, and later Pantages Theatre program. (OHS Collections.)

The Reed Opera House in Salem (above) was a showplace of Oregon's capital city. Theatre on second floor was scene of many Victorian plays. (Cronise photo.)
John F. Cordray's Musee'-Theatre at Third and Yamhill, the "heart of Portland's business district in the 90's." (OHS Collections.)

Interior of the Marquam Grand Theatre, Portland, with a seating capacity of 1,800. Edwin Booth, Mme. Melba, Ellen Terry, and many other notables appeared here. (*Oregonian* photo.)

New Market Theatre as it looked about 1954. Note ornate pillars and iron supports. First Street entrance. (Courtesy Lambert Florin.)

Rules of New Market Theater.

Theater rented subject to the following Rules, which are a part of all contracts:

No smoking, no kerosene, coal oil or any burning fluid allowed to be used as light in any room or part of the Theater, except Candles and Gas, red and blue lights for stage-use from iron pans.

All persons belonging to the troupe or engaged about the stage will enter by the rear stairway and pass out the same way. No person belonging to the troupe will be allowed to pass through the Dress Circle to and from the stage, other than the Manager.

No scenes to be painted out or altered, taken or removed from the Theater, without the written consent of the Proprietor.

No person allowed on the stage of the Theater, other than those belonging to the troupe.

All persons are required to leave the Theater after the performance is closed.

All gentlemen who use Tobacco will be particular to use the spittoons in order to ensure cleanliness on the stage.

In no case will permission be granted to any person or persons to sell any candies, nuts, fruit, &c., in the Theater under forfeiture of contract.

☞ *Rent of Theater includes License, Gas and Cleaning only.*

A. P. ANKENY.

Blanche Bates broke ground for new Heilig Theatre October 14, 1909. Memorable showman Portland's Mayor George L. Baker supervised. (OHS Collections.)
A crowded matinee (below) at the Baker Theatre, about 1908. (OHS Collections.)

Curtain call for the "Pirates of Penzance" at Baker, Oregon, about 1890. (OHS Collections.)

A brilliant scene from "The Tempest," featuring players and distinguished new theatre of Ashland Shakespearean Festival, 1960. (Courtesy Oregon Shakespearean Festival. Classic Studio photo.)

STOCK COMPANIES / *Take Over*

Western stock companies kept most of the engaging qualities which had given character to the young American stage. Such changes as occurred during the migration lent them at times a more rustic face.

Long accepted as the backbone of the theatre anywhere, stock's contribution to the struggling new world stage had been massive. Philadelphia's veteran Walnut Street Theatre, opened in 1809, had schooled immortals. The versatile Drews, Forrest, McCullough —all had faced its footlights. Imported from overseas, the useful stock system also prevailed in Boston, New York and other cities of sufficient size to support a year-round theatre, or one at least playing steadily during the long winter months. Actors bred within its stern tradition leave no doubt as to its sovereign worth.

Otis Skinner in his *Footlights and Spotlights* has a word to say as to its virtues, along with some delightful vignettes of brilliant stars with whom he played: the great ones mentioned, Mary Anderson, the tragic Madame Janauschek, the vivacious Lotta. His own stage apprenticeship took place while the stock system was fading from its ancient footholds. As he puts it: "The season of 1878-79 at the Walnut Street Theatre saw the last of the stock system in that historic house. The system of theatres was changing. Hitherto the custom prevailed of local companies in the larger places—Boston, Philadelphia, Baltimore, Cleveland, Cincinnati, Chicago—and in a few places in the South—to whom came the visiting star with his repertory. When a number of pieces were to be produced, the star's director would precede him (or her) to conduct rehearsals in advance."

These trial runs were conducted by means of what were known as skeleton manuscripts, in which only the cues of the absent star's dialogue were indicated. The resident actors, however, were required to be letter perfect in all texts of their supporting roles; with the current vogue for four and five-act plays this alone entailed feats of memory. The manuscripts were often bare-faced rewrites of popular plays, with little mention of authors. Pirating was common. Standard repertory practice called as well for interpretation of widely different roles in rapid succession — a demanding, gruelling system which nevertheless produced giants on the stage. It fostered swift versatility and sensitive ensemble playing, as against the flatter demands of the dawning star system just then edging it out.

In the Northwest, too often theatre-starved, its pioneer stock companies were a boon. Touring out from the few big-town theatres, they provided much of the dramatic fare of the region. Their stops varied in length; and visiting out-of-state professionals might tarry in the new territory an entire season, as did Julia Dean Hayne. Far from being transients, they ranked as favored citizens—in the leisurely pre-railroad days, that is.

The oldtime stock companies were geared for disaster, which they often met. Doubling—and make-up—produced miracles. A Leading Man, a Leading Woman, an Ingenue and a good stout Villain to garner plentiful hisses were essential. If possible, a Grand Dame, a Light Comedian, a Character Actor and even more ornamental types might be added in the larger troupes. The plays themselves were highly demanding, as earlier noted; the most casual glance at the repertory of such frontier favorites as Mr. and Mrs. F. M. Bates, of Mrs. Phelps or pioneer George Waldron reveals a most ambitious range. Done with the prevailing bravura, they called for great vigor and gusto in speech and gesture. At its best, the stock company fostered genius; its deep roots led to Drury Lane, to the blue-sky Globe; its ranks had known the man Shakespeare, the great Moliere, Burbage and lovely Siddons. At its worst, it could be dull as dishwater, the awful refuge of ranting hams. Versatile as it was, it was in for change.

As the railroads reached long fingers across the land, it became progressively easy to transport whole companies from place to place, stage sets and all, in such hit plays as the fickle public might fancy. Players, orchestra and scenery were whisked from coast to coast as though by magic. The road shows, however, usually featured some reigning star, who might have to play the same role for years, as did Otis Skinner in *Kismet,* much to his bodily harm. Supporting roles and bit parts called for little freshness of acting. For the player, the trend was toward monotony and the stereotyped. But for the harassed manager, it could spell blessed box office—obviously a cheerful aspect of the theatre. Unfortunately, the road show had mongrel relatives.

Most annoying of these were certain run-down "combinations" which during the eighties plagued the entire West Coast. Tawdry ancestors of the later dazzling road shows, their pinch-penny casting, fitted to stale plays, were to trigger a rebellion. Main recruiting ground was New York City. Early established as the dramatic capital of the nation, and undoubted center of its far-flung show business, it was snug haven for homing thespians, battered by disaster or bright with laurels.

Here they hung out at the congenial Union Place Hotel or others nearby. News stories of the day portray these resting lions of the stage, gregarious and extrovert; shabby or splendid as fortune decreed, but all subtly marked by their profession and strangely ageless, perhaps from long frontage on the make-believe. The true artist rubbed elbows with the sham; then as now the more threadbare lodged drably close to 'dramatic bureaus.' And there, between seasons, cagey managers made up their lists for the long trek beyond the Mississippi. More and more, crimped by itching palms, the touring combination became the refuge of the hack actor. No wonder the miles between were strewn with stranded players, beating their way back to Broadway and the bright lights.

The West Coast *Music and Drama,* published in San Francisco and noted for its love of theatre, in its issue of March 7, 1885, remarks: "The system of bringing combinations to the coast is gradually but surely dying out." Following caustic blasts at the system in general, it takes aim at the so-called 'all-star cast' just then holding forth at the Bush Street Theatre—and sadly belying advance notice. "San Francisco," rasps the irate editor, "will respond to nothing less than the first-rate," as even now.

It might be well to observe the favored ammunition of these theatrical heavy guns, all the more since both the touring combinations and the resident stock companies of the day drew from a common reservoir of scripts. Stage techniques were also similar, and plays were slanted for the flow of oratory, the florid gesture demanded by the current Grand Manner. Among a host,

Joaquin Miller's plays are perhaps typical of the prevailing bravura mood.

Definitely rough-hewn products of the dramatic art, the plays for some years eclipsed his welling verse. His first play, *The Danites,* produced in New York (1877), ran for two years with "more than average success." Later taken to England, it was fully as popular there in a long tour following its presentation by the McKee-Rankin Company at Sadler's Wells in 1880. Miller himself had received British acclaim on his visit eight years before, and later flaunted a ring with the magic letters V.R., ostensibly a gift of the queen. Other plays followed. His four-act melodrama, *Mexico,* using quasi-historical events of the time of the Emperor Maximilian, also produced in New York (1879), drew favorable editorial comment from the *Sun.* Its somewhat biased leading lady, "the renowned German-American actress, Miss Van Stamwitz" pronounced him "the greatest playwright since Shakespeare." Only moderately successful, it advanced him on the road to fame. The spotlight of attention growing from lawsuits as to copyrights, plagiarism and other legal aspects attending later dramatic efforts, did him no harm whatever.

Of the seven plays elsewhere listed,* by far the most popular were his two robust Westerns. *The Danites,* dramatized from an earlier short story, "The First Families of the Sierras," depicts the fictional revenge of a group of Mormons for death of their prophet leader, Joseph Smith. Its fellow, *Forty-Nine,* in somewhat less than Bret Harte fashion, presents scenes and characters from gold rush days. Extensively played both in this country and abroad, they became favorite vehicles for combinations or for resident stock. In the hands of McKee-Rankin, results were spectacular.

This well-known actor had created the lead in the highly popular *Two Orphans.* As Sandy in *The Danites,* he scored a heavy success on the road. Finding that the massive star had also absorbed copyrights and box office receipts of the plays, Miller in a success-

---

*Copyright records list Miller's plays as follows: *Mexico,* 1879; *Two Babes in the Wood,* 1880; *O Rare Colorado,* 1881; *Oregon,* 1881; *The Danites,* 1882; *Forty-Nine, the Gold Seekers of the Sierras,* 1882; *Puts, Calls and Straddles,* 1883; *Our Western Cousin,* 1883; *The Silent Man,* 1883; *Tally Ho,* 1883. Both of Miller's major plays, *The Danites,* and *Forty-Nine,* are in four acts.

ful lawsuit established his author's rights, though admitting technical aid from a hack arranger. The court decree, however, specified that the sizable royalties must be collected in person. In this unusual situation, Miller for a time followed the Rankin company on tour, occasionally splitting proceeds with needy troupers. Enough was left to permit him to live in New York for a time, during which with characteristic zest he dashed off several others, all too clearly marked by the journeyman's hand.

The premiere of *The Danites* in his adopted home, San Francisco, was received with definite chill by the critics, despite the friendly presence of George Sterling, Ina Coolbrith and other literary lights. The cast assembled at the town's leading theatre, the Baldwin, was impressive: famous McKee-Rankin and his able wife, supported by Annie Pixley, a rising artist. Its durable plot, however, intrigued the public, and together with *Forty-Nine,* it was widely produced in this country, in England, Australia—and, quite naturally, the Northwest. A long run of *The Danites,* starring Rankin, is reported at the New Market in 1882; in October of that year, Miller watched its production from a stage box at Seattle's Third Avenue Theatre. The last year of the decade saw both plays on the boards in main theatres, throughout the Northwest as elsewhere.

One production, "sponsored by the poet's friends and classmates," was given at his home town, Eugene, in 1894, by the touring Stutz Company. Even at this late date, local reaction to Miller's poetry was notably reluctant. Chosen as visiting lion at Pendleton, Oregon, for its Fourth of July celebration of 1896, he was there to read his narrative poem, "Song of the Sierras." Admitting him "a rhymester of unusual glow," the advance notice cautiously adds "though he is perhaps better known as the author of *The Danites*." The two Miller creations, wordy and melodramatic, played on through the nineties, fading with their era.

Good companies as well as poor ones were on the road, and good plays as well. A fine troupe of English athletes and jugglers did a rushing business, as did the better acting groups. And, such as they were, Northwest theatres vied for the combinations. Seattle's Frye's Opera House advertised itself, in 1885, as "The only Combination Theatre in the Territory," and as "Playing all suitable

Combinations." They, however, were increasingly rare; in protest, certain West Coast organizations took to the road, with pleasing results. The able Grismer-Davies Combination, formed in San Francisco, turned in during 1888 "The longest season on record. Six months en route and still going." At Portland's New Market, at popular prices, they set a record of eleven weeks' playing, together with "The most profitable season on the Puget Sound circuit." The public loved plays, and business was booming. It was at this juncture that the stock companies took over.

Plainly, better results for both actors and public could be achieved by professional groups resident at the larger playhouses. With proper time for rehearsals, adequate backstage facilities and a skilled director, greater finish was possible. The public could enjoy a planned series of standard plays, staged with rewarding care. The actors, as pointed out by *Music and Drama,* could "have homes like other people" —no mean factor. Spurred by the shoddy output of many road shows, resident professionals became worthy and formidable rivals.

The range of the resident stock companies was greatly widened when, in the fading eighties, Cordray's Portland Musee' Troupe began trading stages with his Seattle stock group. Both towns enjoyed their mutual stars, the lively Tittell Sisters and popular R. E. French. Cordray's Seattle Musee', later its veteran Third Avenue Theatre, was to provide that city for years with wholesome dramatic fare. In Portland, such standard favorites as *Leah the Forsaken, The Streets of London, Dora,* or *Lady Audley's Secret* might be weekly viewed. In two Irish plays, *Erin Go Bragh* and *Kathleen Mavourneen,* vivacious Minnie Tittell gave her celebrated Loie Fuller serpentine dance, for lengthy billings.

The Portland group, touring out to smaller towns, relived the hazards of the early troupers. Taking the road briefly during an engagement of the Calhoun Opera Company in 1893 at the Portland Cordray, they visited the upper valley in midwinter, playing in Oregon City, Salem, Albany, Eugene and Corvallis. Along with heavy colds, they brought back dire tales of drafty halls, poor stages, chilly dressing rooms. At one place they were obliged to dress at the hotel and walk in costume through deep snow to their stage. Such was the trouper's checkered life.

The building of Portland's modern Marquam Grand in 1889, with special backstage equipment for the larger road shows, gave a strong assist to the travelling companies. At the makeshift Cordray's, stock had drifted into dull days. Fading, it edged briefly into the spotlight with a suit for breach of contract against the polished Frawley Stock Company of New York. Originally billed at Cordray's for a two-week run in 1896, they had by-passed it for the alluring stage equipment of the newer theatre. Rising star in the Frawley ensemble was young Blanche Bates, back for a turn in her birthplace.

Much longer lived, and more famous, was the stock company attached to Cordray's Seattle Musee'. Washington, a younger territory more slowly visited by travelling actors, was perhaps for that reason more indebted to its resident players. Trailbreakers for a long line of dependable stage folk attached to the renamed Third Avenue, this early playing group deserves an accolade.

When John Cordray, victim of the depression of '93, withdrew to the south, his Seattle Musee' fell into capable hands. Local managers William Russell and Edward Drew, at first managing the playhouse for a creditor bank, had somehow kept it solvent. By shrewd appraisal of public taste and devoted care, they had there established that long hierarchy of resident groups which under changing names carried on until far down in the present century.

Outriding disaster, the veteran theatre had kept its marquee' bright. With the gold rush of 1897, the scene had changed. The town's horizon had swiftly widened. When versatile John P. Howe was called back from New York to guide the fortunes of its newly built Seattle Theatre, his first move was to import an eastern stock company, the Manhattan Players, direct from Broadway. The *New York Mirror* commented as follows: "Seattle has been pretty shabbily treated of late in the matter of travelling companies. There is hardly a city of Seattle's size in the East where stock companies do not exist and are popular." The *Mirror* further predicted that if such resident groups could make headway where opposed by the best travelling attractions, they must undoubtedly succeed "against theatrical attractions that can not be booked elsewhere." Therein lay the crux of the sharp conflict between shoddy road show and resident stock—dynamite for an approaching explosion.

Though the urban Manhattan Company lasted but a season, its finished efforts drew high praise from the press and from passing visitors. It also helped to create a favorable climate for the long line of Seattle stock companies to follow. Fresh from Broadway was its suave star, Ralph Stuart. "Compared with Ralph Stuart," the Seattle *Argus* of January 2, 1902, declared, "Tim Farley is a farmer and James Neill a rank amateur." At season's end, however, actor Stuart was lured south by rising tycoon George L. Baker to head his new-formed Portland group, for spring billings. Results were spectacular, and the augmented Baker Players in turn played Seattle from April 2 through June 20 of 1903, as well as March and April of 1904.

In Seattle, meanwhile, Manager Russell during a New York visit in June of 1905, recharged his old Third Avenue by "an entirely new company, including author and producer." This was the historic Taylor Stock Company whose leading lady, Laurette Taylor, was to leave the American stage some poignant memories. The Taylors, after a summer season at the Third Avenue, held over for much of the winter of 1906 also. But they too were lured by Baker to Portland, where Laurette made a spectacular hit in *The King of The Opium Ring*. Ralph Stuart had by now returned to New York. Miss Taylor also went East not long after. There, wedded to another playwright, Hartley Manners, she achieved Broadway fame in a play written by him for her, *Peg O' My Heart,* at friend John Cort's new theatre. The way west was by now familiar to eastern stock companies.

Throughout Seattle's later swift growth, its loyal love of stock continued. When the aging Seattle Theatre was relinquished by Manager Howe to the more militant hand of John Cort, the latter routed major road shows at his more splendid blue plush opera house. Stock was billed at the Seattle, renamed the President. In one of its perennial remodellings, it was in 1910 re-opened by the Baker Stock Company of Portland. The realism of their offering, *On the Bridge at Midnight,* drew startled comment. On stage appeared "a steamer with lights, its funnel pouring out smoke, and encrusted with ice." It was a typical Baker *tour de force*.

Stock was played also at the Alcazar; Russell and Drew had opened the Lyric for the same purpose. Alexander Pantages, beginning his fabulous career, had built his sole legitimate theatre, the Lois, expressly for stock. Designed for the family trade, it was eminently successful from its opening on October 7, 1906 until destroyed by fire four years later. Stock had firmly grounded itself in the Northwest, not only for summer replacements, but for year-round playing.

Much as the town loved its faithful players, only a few of them achieved distinction. It was, however, in Seattle, as Guthrie McClintic recalls in his memoirs, *Kit and I*, that he succumbed to the spell of the theatre—at the age of twelve, while watching "a bewitching young lady named Laurette Taylor." At the moment she was adorning stock in a series of melodramas with such inciting titles as *Escape from the Harem*, and *Stolen from the Gypsies*. Strong magic indeed!

Stalwarts at the old Seattle Theatre for a time were Guy Bates Post, of later *Masquerader* fame, and his then wife, Sarah Truax. The latter, starred in the *Garden of Allah* and kindred drama, returned to share actively in the town's dramatic affairs. In general, however, the Seattle stock companies used very few imported stars.

In her interesting *History of Seattle Stock Companies from the Beginning to 1934,* Mary K. Rohrer cites the above fact* as one of the reasons for their decline. Mentioned also is their habit of staying rather close to home—a trait by no means shared by southern confreres. In almost forty years of operation, the writer notes, playbills reveal only a few guest players. Instead, team work was stressed. A growing shortage of good plays available to stock aggravated the situation. This was everywhere true, though the pattern here designated as "Western stock" happily did not prevail south of the Columbia. Despite nagging difficulties, the service of the Seattle stock companies was long and distinguished. It was not until late in 1933 that the last of them took

*Mary K. Rohrer, *A History of Seattle's Stock Companies from Their Beginnings to 1934* (University of Washington Press, 1945), 37.

their final bow at the Moore Theatre, ending forty-four years of useful existence.

It remained, however, for a master showman, George L. Baker, to create the region's most brilliant stock company, which functioned far beyond local bounds. Known along the entire West Coast, its life spanned the best years of the American theatre; its saga contains elements of that Horatio Alger story so dear to the national heart. For we must at once credit some of its special qualities to the temper of its founder.

Young Baker, driven always by a nagging passion for the stage, rose from early hardship to a "walk on" job at San Francisco's Morosco Theatre, and was soon bossing backstage work at that musty old playhouse. New scenes called him north. Failing to find work at Seattle during lean years, he did a turn at tending the animals at Cordray's Portland Musee', also playing bit parts on stage. In quick succession, after the opening of the Marquam Grand in 1889, he was technician in charge of stage sets, scene shifts and lighting; lithographer responsible for outdoor publicity; and assistant to Calvin Heilig, good friend with whom he was long associated.

Ambitious and restless in trouper fashion, he leased the brand new opera house at Baker City, just then on the rebound from a boom. In the proverbial bust that so often follows, Baker, as he himself phrased it, "lost his shirt," returning to Portland practically bankrupt. There too Cordray's Musee' — now called the Metropolitan — was in dire straits. By devoted care, Baker eased the wobbly Wiedemann Stock Company through a bare season, later bringing in new players in free-lance offerings off the beaten track. Among these, Laurette Taylor in *The King of the Opium Ring* tapped a gold mine that put Baker well back on his financial feet. From the first—and characteristically—Baker favored guest stars in the manner of eastern stock, thus departing radically from the easier patterns favored north of the Columbia.

Succeeding offerings—minstrel shows, variety and vaudeville attractions spiced by an occasional melodrama—were also successful. With enough cash for the formation of his own group of players, the flimsy so-called Metropolitan Theatre (Cordray's) was renamed the Baker in 1901. It was at this time that Baker induced able Ralph Stuart to take over the direction of his remodelled theatre for the 1902 season. With thorough knowledge of the stage, Stuart imported a group of stellar players, among them Catherine Countiss, Lansing Rowan, Frank Sherman, Elizabeth Stewart and others. Their ten-week season scored a complete artistic and financial success in such dramas as *The Silver King*, *In Old Mizzouri*, *Monte Cristo*, *The Westerner* and *The Lost Paradise*.

On Stuart's return to New York, Baker negotiated with James Neill and Oliver Morosco of California for organization of a new stock company to take on where Stuart left off. The Neill Stock Company brought to Portland a number of important players including Charles Wingate, William Bernard, Robert Morris, Howard Russell, William Dills, Elsie Esmond, Lillian Rhodes, Elspeth McNeill, and the Gleasons, William and Mina. Their lively repertoire offered *Lady Windermere's Fan*, *Mr. Barnes of New York*, *The Girl I Left Behind Me*, *A Social Highwayman*, *The Christian*, *The Wife*, *A Contented Woman* and *The Masqueraders*—all plays of the urban type.

The *Oregon Journal* of May 7, 1933, recalls: "The Baker Stock Company in early 1903 was made up from the cast of the Neill Company, with additions from time to time." A list of later players follows, together with their offerings, among them *Men and Women*, *Facing the Music* (with James J. Corbett), *The Great Diamond Robbery* and *Shenandoah*.

A brilliant season headed by John Sainpolis of later film fame met with like success. Featured in this talented group were Lillian Lawrence and daughter, Ellen Gray Terry, Howard Russell, Mabel Seymour, the Gleason family, Louise Kent and Fay Bainter. Sainpolis too returned to New York, but other stars took over— Franklin Underwood, Frances Slossom. Donal Boles ("In and out of the company two or three times," by Baker's own statement), Gertrude Rivers and the ever-popular Gleasons, Mina, William and son James.

"The Baker Stock Company was a hit from the start," the *Journal* continues, "and it was in turn the organization that was to form the backbone of Portland's entertainment for the next ten or twelve years." It was also school for many actors shortly to shine on the national stage, Izetta Jewel, leading lady for Otis Skinner, Fay Bainter, Florence and Theodore Roberts and the unforgettable Laurette among these. Juvenile apprentice actors were John Gilbert, son of Ida Adair and William Gilbert, young James Gleason of that footlight family. A long list of screen or radio notables there put on make-up: one-time lumberjack Clark Gable, suave William Powell, Jean Hersholt, Mary Boland. Comedian Edward Everett Horton was a strong favorite; Verna Felton shone in dime stock, her father manager of the Lyric.

Somewhat later, in the '20s, tiny Mayo Methot, on stage at four, was a child star in *The Littlest Rebel*. An ingenue at thirteen, she moved to Broadway to play leads in *The Song-and-Dance Man,* with George M. Cohan (1924), *The Torch Song, Half Gods* and other successes, before her marriage to Humphrey Bogart. The roster of newer stock companies in the present century, the Forrest Taylor Players or Duffy Stock Company, yields a lengthy list of alumni.

Major stars of the American stage, billed often at the town's early theatres, returned with pleasure as more modern playhouses were built — Minnie Maddern Fiske, Blanche Bates, James A. Herne. Following the trail of Cordray and John P. Howe, Baker visited Broadway often in search of new talent. Oregon's love of tradition may have had a hand in the matter, but there the so-called "Eastern stock" pattern was always followed, using many guest stars, and with a fondness for travel. The Baker Players had frequent summer billings in San Francisco; they toured assiduously, exchanging often with Seattle. The combination of a manager's daring and Oregon's innate taste had happy results for the town.

A shrewd man of the theatre, Baker began in Portland the sale of season tickets, at thrifty rates. Avid fans often waited all night in line to assure favored seats, with Baker himself providing blankets and coffee. Stressing family theatre, as had Cordray before him, plays were chosen with care. Scandals among players were frowned upon. Many of them, living for years in the town, attracted loyal friends and fans. Their record of service to the town, as well as the Baker *esprit de corps,* is legendary, and tinged with affection. Working relations between players and manager were excellent. There were frequent meetings before production, for reading of scripts and suggestions as to interpretations of roles.

An easy spender, Baker spared no expense in staging chosen plays. As these were quite often current Broadway hits, for special occasions money flowed forth. For the opening of his new Bungalow Theatre, he chose Belasco's smash hit, *The Girl of the Golden West*—a play, by the way, which also broke records for the longest run of a play in Portland. Current vehicle of now famous Blanche Bates, and with soaring royalties, his output staggered even friend Calvin Heilig, himself a manager. It also perhaps explains in part why Baker left the theatre a bankrupt. His backstage experience led him to realism in sets. Some of his more startling effects have been related. On one occasion an entire reassembled schoolhouse was moved to Seattle, for proper background.

The long list of Baker offerings during the years must be omitted. Tragedy, comedy, light opera, melodrama—even vaudeville were all essayed. In its March 1, 1907, issue, the *Spectator,* a weekly journal given to searching comments on the fine arts, commends his production of *Leah Kletchna,* a tragedy. Two light operas, *The Red Mill* and *Old Heidelberg,* followed in quick succession. On April 16, *The Admirable Crichton* was presented for the first time on the Pacific Coast. Soon after, reviewing a production of Hall Caine's *Prodigal Son,* the *Spectator's* literate editor, Hugh Hume, remarks: "There is nothing George L. Baker will not attempt with his company. Once in a while Baker relapses into an indifferent play, but often it gives something new and consequential. *The Prodigal Son* is a feather in the cap of the stock concern."

Two smaller theatres, the Lyric and the Star, were shortly acquired for presentation of dime stock—a far cry indeed from days of struggle at the old Third Street playhouse. In a growing dearth of suitable theatres, Baker, as he put it, "moved around a good deal." As told by the *Rose City Magazine* for September, 1908: "George L. Baker, Portland's most restless and progressive theatre manager, has taken another whirl at the wheel of the city's amusement situation, and moved his popular players, widely known as the Baker Stock Company, from the old Third Street location where they have held forth for so long, uptown to the swell district of upper Morrison, and established themselves permanently in the elegant new Bungalow at the corner of Twelfth. The Bungalow is the old Empire remodelled, and the transformation from a gloomy cavern to a bright airy place of beauty and delight is something to marvel at."

Fresh plastered walls, panellings of polished natural wood, a ventilating system and freedom from dust 'germs' indeed worked wonders for the one-time Tabernacle, which had housed both revivals and horse shows. Its triumphant opening on September 27, presenting "for the first time on the Pacific Coast" Belasco's *Girl of the Golden West,* with sparkling Izetta Jewel in the lead, delighted patrons, as did later offerings. "Portland," the article continues, "is a good show town. Eight theatres slating regular dramatic, musical and vaudeville attractions, beside the host of motion picture houses . . . all doing good business . . . causes one to think there are more nearly 250,000 people than the 150,000 people here."

A brand-new theatre, built nearby at Eleventh and Morrison two years later at a reputed cost of $70,000, gave further room for experiment. Described as "one of the largest on the coast," it accommodated many more patrons. For the opening of the New Baker Theatre on September 18, 1910, star Izetta Jewel, now leading lady for Otis Skinner, returned to launch a rousing season of dràma agreeably spiced with light opera. This durable playhouse was in later years home for newer stock aggregations, among them the Forrest Taylor Players. As the Dufwin, it functioned for the Duffy Stock Company. Rechristened the Playhouse, it housed many touring companies as well; and as a motion picture house and catch-all assembly, survived until 1956.

Baker's Stock Company had often been billed in San Francisco; at this point it moved north as well. Currently managing the Bungalow for good friend Heilig, Baker established resident stock groups at Seattle and Spokane. The year 1910, as later noted, was a crucial one for West Coast managers. The approaching Syndicate Rebellion had caused much ferment. It witnessed also the building of the handsome Heilig Theatre, at which the larger road shows might now be staged. Baker, by gentlemen's agreement—and taste —continued in his chosen field of family theatre.

At popular prices, he served a town-wide clientele, losing no theatrical tricks. With his stage know-how and strong flair for realism, moving bridges, locomotives, steamboats were conjured up, as noted. Melodrama had by no means faded. At Cordray's, during a showing of the oldtime thriller, *Blue Jeans,* details of the sawmill scene, where the strapped hero is slowly drawn toward the fatal buzz-saw, had called forth cat-calls from critical lumberjacks. No such fiasco would satisfy Baker. In a Seattle production, he had a huge tank sunk beneath the stage for the hero's death leap. Fond of experiment, he made the first use of the motion picture on the stage thereabouts. This was for the play, *In Old Kentucky,* where results of a furious horse race must be visible. For another play, he evoked an entire Chinese village. His strong feeling for local backgrounds prompted his production of the three-act play, *Oregon,* by June Ordway, and *The Alaskan,* by Joseph Blethen. Audiences profited by their changing variety, though the impulsive manager at times lost.

At its peak, the so-called Baker Enterprises included, about 1914, not only the parent stock company in Portland but two out-of-town branches. One, located at the Seattle Theatre, had Ernest Shipman as manager; a second at Spokane, Washington, was directed by able Franklin Underwood. In home-town Portland, two theatres were operated: the Baker, "New, modern, strictly fireproof, seats 1,600," and the Bungalow, "Empire Theatre Company, lessees, playing the popular price attractions of the Northwestern Theatrical Association." President of the latter organization was Calvin Heilig, with John Cort as general manager. A New York office in the Knickerbocker Theatre Annex was also listed, citing affiliations with Belasco and Mayer in that city, and with the Oliver Morosco and Burbank Stock Company in Los Angeles. Cordray appears as a member of the organization, attesting the solidarity now achieved by Northwest managers— and, in particular, the wide reach possible for the resident stock company.

The Baker Stock Company functioned actively between 1901 and 1922, and at intervals later. Under Baker's personal guidance for seventeen years, in fading it retained the name, if not the spirit, of its founder. His final stance was at the rebuilt Marquam Grand at Sixth and Morrison. Renamed the Baker, it served for several years, presenting both road shows and stock. But for Baker, width had not brought depth, and change was everywhere rampant. When he withdrew to politics, around 1915 — he had been councilman for eleven years — he filed a petition in bankruptcy. All debts, however, were later carefully paid off, and to politics he devoted the same restless energy. From city commissioner, he became the city's almost permanent mayor. Nor did the showman's flair desert him in this sixteen-year role. His now legendary greetings of Queen Marie of Roumania, of singer Mary Garden and fellow mayor James Walker furnished lively copy for newsmen, while keeping the home town well in the spotlight. His interest in civic affairs was, however, undoubtedly genuine and productive, backed by an informal gift for leadership. As for the theatre, he must remain one of the Northwest's most dynamic figures.

Checkered days for his stock company followed his exit. At the Sixth Street Baker, friends Pearl, Seaman and Wood carried on for a time. Later, the Baker Enterprises, purchased by Wood, Everett and Zetosch in 1917, for two seasons presented musical comedies, aided by transient stock groups. Under the name of the Alcazar Players, they shifted about as needed. When the Forrest Taylor Players moved into the remodelled Heilig (currently the Orpheum), the chameleon Baker Musical Stock Company held forth at Morrison Street for a time, before retreating to the smaller Lyric . . . But show business was by now being crowded by motion pictures and vaudeville. Last incarnation, with the capable Duffy Stock Company as rivals, was in a group calling themselves the Baker Players, who for some years presented radio plays. By the time of Baker's death in 1941 the scene had completely changed and an era had ended.

There was both wisdom and regret in the maestro's words, not long before his death. "In the old days when actors were actors and plays were plays," he observed,* "there was also a discrimi-

---

*Interview with George L. Baker, April, 1941 at Seaside, Oregon.

nating public. It is of course obvious that a large city like New York is also a great production center. And there, where thousands of people are gathered for various reasons, one could always get a theatre full of people to witness plays. Whereas if given out here for one or two nights only it was more of a risk. Stock companies had to be very careful in their selections. Mistakes were expensive.

"But what built up show business in this country as in England—in other words what made actors—was the stock company. Their long-lasting stars, say in the hands of Frohman, maintained the highest type of acting. And on tour they packed the house because there was variety in their repertoire. Such actors as Kyrle Bellew, Mrs. Brown Potter or Richard Mansfield always had several solid offerings." Asked for his favorite actor, he named the younger Salvini, "had he lived," for his marvellous skill and brilliance; his preference for plays was for those of the Frohman type.

As to the stock company and its sovereign worth to the theatre, many another actor and director, both in this country and overseas, have echoed the same words.

Off-stage dynasts in the Northwest theatre scene notably altered its range and direction; in part, they framed its tastes. Men of action, they built its playhouses, hired its actors, and in general ran its workaday business—not without a prudent finger on its vital pulse: box office. These were the managers—its tycoons, if you will.

Freshman efforts of a few dominant figures have been lightly sketched in. Their more mature achievements, affecting the life of the region, must now receive a word.

One transition figure, John P. Howe, entered from the East in the '80s, as manager of eminent tragedian W. E. Sheridan. Theatre-wise and cultured, Howe gave to Portland's New Market Theatre some of its more brilliant days, before taking over at the informal Casino. His spirited duels with rival manager Beede to the north set the tempo of the times; as close friend of wealthy Judge Marquam he suggested the building of the more splendid Marquam Grand, and he had a finger in plans for Spokane's modern Auditorium Theatre. Later, as owner and operator of playhouses in Seattle and San Francisco, he was for some years arbiter of the entire Northwestern circuit. By residence in the Sound cities and those farther south, he knew the region and its needs.

As top man along the West Coast, he arranged the billing of the traveling combinations until 1891, and aside from brief interludes, his domination of the theatrical scene thereabouts continued until the present century. By alliance with former rival Beede, of Squire's Opera House at Seattle, he had assured wider booking of all road shows. Called back from a temporary New York residence, he became in 1895 manager of Seattle's impressive opera house. The Alpha Theatre of Tacoma was also under his banner for a time.

A frequent visitor to New York and devoted lover of good plays, he early protested the shoddy offerings sent westward. As early as 1904, Howe announced his withdrawal from the eastern syndicate, and together with fellow manager George Baker of Portland and others, joined in a new organization, the West Coast Independent Managers' Association. Controlling about twenty theatres, they planned to bill their own selected attractions, filling in with resident stock as needed. John Cort, later militant leader of the Independents, still lingered with the syndicates as their western representative.

The movement was, however, premature, as the group could not muster enough paying attractions. In 1905, with great reluctance, Howe withdrew from the northern scene, concentrating on man·· agement of his two San Francisco theatres, the Alcazar and Stockwell, which he had operated profitably since their acquisition ten years before. The Seattle theatre, leased to Cort, was added to the syndicate string, thus leaving the town without an independent theatre. Excavations had begun on a fine playhouse, the Alhambra, at Fourth and Pine, but this too was sold.

Howe's withdrawal from the northern scene brought a public letter of regret from New York manager Harrison Grey Fiske. In this he lauded Howe's "long and splendid fight in the interest of the Independents," adding that "adherence to principle is something rare in theatre management." Howe is remembered for bringing to his Seattle playhouse such luminaries as Bernhardt, Sothern, Warfield and Mrs. Fiske. At Portland he set an urban pattern. His innate good taste and independence strongly molded the stage of his day. Failing health had been a factor in his retirement, followed by his death in Eugene in 1910.

A transition figure also is that of John F. Cordray, sponsor in the Northwest of the hybrid musee' theatre. Profitable operation of his two theatres so named brought a neat fortune, promptly lost in the depression of '93. Having acquired also Tacoma's Alpha Theatre, a bank failure there caused retreat to his original Musee' at Portland. With the purchase of the Alpha, however, beginnings of a Northwest circuit had been pushed by Cordray, later woven into a far-flung web by fellow managers Hanna, Cort and Heilig.

Cordray's Portland Musee' Players deserve a word as a pioneer group who in their own right helped to achieve modern techniques. Playbills of the early '90s at Cordray's list well-seasoned guest players: W. H. Lytell, assisted by his wife, Blanche Morrison; Walter Hodges, Aubrey Boucicault with Victory Bateman, niece of Edwin Booth; Frank Bacon in *The Vendetta;* Milton and Dolly Nobles in a popular season that included some of the actor's own plays. Also presented were Belasco's *May Blossom; Around the World in Eighty Days; The Naiad Queen,* a costumed spectacle; and the melodrama, *After Dark.* The famous musical extravaganza, *The Black Crook,* was given in both towns. Notable was a season of opera by the Calhoun Opera Company, whose forty members were brought back in person by Cordray from an eastern tour.

On his withdrawal to the south, Cordray, along with his Portland theatres, leased the newly built Grand at Salem—long a major stop for the better road shows. During Howe's New York residence, Cordray was given charge of all Oregon billings. Until well down in the nineties, most reigning stars played under his banner. He also assumed management of the New Park (Casino) Theatre relinquished by Howe. Remodelled, as the Grand or Cordray's, it functioned as Portland's leading theatre until the splendid Marquam Grand snatched away the road shows. Chief rivals were such informal music halls as the Tivoli.

Cordray, however, moved with the times. The new century had brought a brisk upsurge of vaudeville; in its succeeding evolution from slapstick variety into the more restrained forms, Cordray's firm beliefs as to the quality of stage offerings were highly potent. He now became their active agent. His Portland Grand, sold to John Considine, was an early link in the latter's chain across the nation. Considine, in fact, later set its Northwestern debut there, though its major growth and impulse belong to the Sound country. As the Empress, under management of Keating and Flood, the much-remodelled Grand long remained a vaudeville stronghold.

Cordray in his later days became a valued contact man for the expanding Sullivan-Considine interest, sent wherever an effective organizer was needed. A quiet, courtly man, poised and witty, legend retains many tales of his encounters with temperamental stars; employees recall his courtesy and firm insistence on the stage standards set forth on every theatre program. As vice-president of the Northwest Theatre Owners' Association, he served along with

George Baker, Calvin Heilig and other policy makers of the region until his sudden death in 1935. He had done much to form its growing tastes.

Czar of an ample demesne was Calvin A. Heilig, a shrewd manipulator of off-stage affairs for a half-century of the theatre's most effulgent years. Houses in seven states bore his name, in a wide arc radiating from the West Coast. Never an actor, he built and planned with telling force.

A lucky real estate deal, soon after he came west in 1889, made him owner of the handsome Tacoma Theatre, heart of a profitable business block. Soon after, he assumed management of the still more splendid Marquam Grand at Portland. This he took over from its original San Francisco lessees, Hayman and Friedlander. The former, pockets jingling, was at the moment departing for Broadway, to become a key figure in the lively battle for Northwest bookings. Valued aide to Heilig in his new venture was youthful George Baker. Baker's vital role in Northwest theatre has been related in connection with his famous stock company.

Heilig soon began collecting theatres elsewhere in the Northwest. One of his earliest acquisitions was at Eugene, a river town reaching for urban manners. Seat of the state's university, it had long outgrown its decrepit Rhinehart's Opera House, a flimsy upstairs firetrap. By lease, Heilig acquired a solid brick structure just then being put up by aspiring citizens. The Eugene Theatre, later renamed for its lessee, was given a resounding opening by the Baker Players on November 17, 1903, starring Catherine Countiss in Hall Caine's *The Christian*.

Both Heilig and Baker were present for the occasion, a gala social event attended by the town's elite, decked out in evening garb. It was also marked by a near-fire, caused by overzealous stoking of a downstairs furnace. Baker, appearing onstage, calmed the panicky audience; the small blaze was extinguished, and the play moved to triumphant climax. Until well down in the present century, practically all major companies paused over night at this good show town. Mrs. Fiske, George Arliss, Walter Hampden, Sothern and Marlowe, a host of musical comedies and straight dramas played there. The Baker Players visited often; local dramatics were lively. Done out in fashionable red plush, the Heilig was seldom dark for a full forty years, functioning through the rise of vaudeville and the fuzzy days of the silent films. Remodelled for motion pictures in 1950, the durable structure is still in daily use.

The Heilig circuit soon absorbed many such theatres, both in nearby valley towns and farther north. At Seattle, Heilig acquired an interest in the newly built Alhambra, one of its major playhouses. With his Midas touch, he became a formidable ally for northern tycoon John Cort, in the approaching battle for Northwest autonomy.

In metropolitan Portland, Heilig with clairvoyant timing had in 1906 sold out his interest in the Marquam Grand, currently in need of extensive repairs, and not long after closed by collapse of a nearby sidewall. Following the city's uptown trend, Heilig repeated his financial success at a smaller theatre out at 14th and Washington, the Belasco, alias the Portland. This, renamed the Heilig, sheltered the higher-priced road shows with friend Baker at the helm in the stock and "family" theatres. The reconstructed Marquam Grand, dear to the Portland public, later resumed its road show billing under outside management, and still later housed the peripatetic Baker Players for an interim, until leased for vaudeville by Considine's Orpheum circuit.

Though all coast towns had notably prospered in the nineties, Portland, devoted lover of good theatre, was putting up with some very sorry playhouses—all, however, doing good business. For the road shows, there were only the transient Columbia (Belasco-Portland-Heilig, several times rechristened) and the revamped Bungalow, also thriftily added by Heilig to his widening string. Baker held temporary stance at the jacked-up Marquam Grand; vaudeville claimed a few minor theatres. The cave-in of its fine Marquam Grand had left the town without a proper theatre. Heilig, alive to civic need—and fully conscious of business possibilities—decided to build a theatre worthy of a metropolis.

This he did—and with a flourish. The handsome structure which bore his name for fully half a century—"the finest theatre west of Denver"—was not only lavish but completely modern, fit for the largest touring companies and the greatest artists. Built at a decisive moment, it became the keystone for the Northwest's maturing circuit. Not only did it mark the turning point in a heady conflict, it served as well as castle for a hospitable owner, host to many eminent visitors.

Into its building Heilig put much of his own substantial fortune. This, by astute fund raising, was swelled by contributions from fellow townsmen to assure the half million dollars needed for its completion by 1910. First ground was broken by Portland-born Blanche Bates on October 14, 1909. Its cornerstone was laid, with elaborate ceremony, on July 22, 1910, by Minnie Maddern Fiske, an independent actress much loved by Northwest audiences. It was given a brilliant opening on October 10 following by Viola Allen in *The White Sister*. Thereafter its playbills list all major productions then current on the American stage.

The builder's good taste and imagination were apparent throughout. On its opening, Broadway's Max Figman was to pronounce it "One of the best theatres I've seen, East or West; and for architecture, the most beautiful I've seen." Typical of the Heilig hospitality was his first-night party of 250 distinguished guests invited from all over the Northwest. But, lover of good theatre as well as finance, Heilig forbade the auctioning of seats, which had soared to $100 on the New Market's opening night. Instead, downstairs admissions were pegged at a stable $4, so that the general public might enjoy the event.

The new theatre was fireproof, thus answering the town's outcry against wooden theatres. Its handsome decor and restrained taste pleased sophisticated patrons; players enjoyed its ample working areas, comfortable dressing rooms and modern lighting. Thus in tune with its day, for its initial season a truly dazzling array of artists had been rounded up by the combined independent managers. The plethoric list included Maxine Elliott, Madame Nazimova, Bertha Kalish, James Powers in *Havana*, Sothern and Marlowe in repertory, Jefferson de Angelis in *The Beauty Spot*, to say nothing of James J. Hackett, Frederick Warde, William Faversham, Wilton Lackaye, Walker Whiteside, Margaret Illington, Marie Dressler, and Julian Eltinge. Such alluring light operas as *The Chocolate Soldier, The Merry Widow,* an all-star cast in *The Mikado,* Blanche Ring in *The Yankee Girl* and a new musical by Henry Savage spiced a lively ensemble. The impressive counter-list of the syndicates, drawn from a heavy backlog of attractions, is elsewhere recorded.

The timely building of the modern Heilig made it the deciding factor in the current battle of the region's managers for free choice in selection of plays sent out to the West. Acquiring more and more theatres by lease or purchase, Heilig flourished in his southern empire. He succeeded John Cort as president of the Independent Northwest Theatrical Association, and soon owned theatres in 200 towns of seven states. Plays leaving New York could be given a full year's billing, playing only in Heilig-controlled theatres.

A lavish executive suite built into the heart of Heilig's Portland playhouse did double duty for work or entertainment. The huge work table ceded space to hunting trophies, Oriental rugs and many signed portraits of famous actors. Added were a small salon, dining room and kitchen; on a balcony, above, a pipe organ with pushbutton control designed by the host. In the guest rooms, still higher, fourposters and antiques. And, topping all, reached by separate winding stairway, a private viewing-box looked far down on a stage where in the golden age of the theatre, the nation's finest actors faced its footlights. During his frequent absences in New York, in Europe or his country place at American Lake near Tacoma, the suite would be turned over, carte blanche, to visiting friends.

Heilig's main interest remained always with the legitimate stage and its more polished performance. As the road shows lagged, and with failing health, he retained only his Portland theatre. This, under changing names—the Dufwin, the Mayfair—became the stronghold of resident stock, though still billing such road shows as were abroad. Ranking for many years as the town's main legitimate theatre, it was host to contemporary stars Helen Hayes, Katherine Cornell, Maurice Evans, Ethel Barrymore and many others, with part-time use for motion pictures. Remodelled in 1955, it is now the Fox Theatre.

Even in partial retirement Heilig retained the use of his Portland suite until his death in 1941. Though that of longtime associate George Baker occurred a few weeks earlier, he was not told of the passing of a friend. Neither perhaps sensed the passing of an era.

Colorful as a carnival hat was the career of aggressive John Cort, builder and battler. A big, jovial Irishman with a flair for off-beat practical jokes, he found the informal frontier much to his liking when he arrived from the East at eighteen—a stranded actor. Seattle, a rawboned sawmill town in 1887, frankly enjoyed its long skid road and noisy box houses. But the young town's boundless vigor matched his own; the Sound's salty air was tonic. The newcomer's stout love of good theatre was later to leave its mark.

He soon took over the Standard, a waterfront variety theatre, but during complete overhauling brought in new and better performers to replace the usual hodge-podge, studded by slipshod aggregations in such dramatic die-hards as *Hazel Kirke, Peck's Bad Boy* or *Fun on the Bristol*. Some very good actors were beginning to stray north, even a few opera companies. With no illusions as to the tastes of his majority audience—transients all—Cort at fancy salaries imported offerings more satisfying to the growing number of solid citizens. An easy spender, his brand-new Standard, elegant for its day, was finished early in 1889, brave with electric lights, proscenium boxes—and a long bar ordered from Chicago. Cort was doing fine when on a sudden June day a flaming glue pot down street abruptly changed the scene. In the holocaust which destroyed the town's major business center, all its theatres, including Cort's new Standard, were burned.

Impulsive and warm-hearted, Cort at once set up a large tent to feed the hungry crowds, and fourteen days later, on a hastily built stage, resumed at the so-called Standard the Third. By November, Cort again had permanent quarters in his resurgent fourth Standard Theatre. Its structure was substantial, and in addition to the usual florid fare, playbills announced "A special grand Matinee every Saturday for Ladies and Children." With forthright vision, Cort began organizing playing circuits, and by 1890 could offer performers "16 weeks billing in Butte, Spokane,

Seattle, Portland, San Francisco and a few smaller places." At Portland, the durable Tivoli became the new Cort's Standard.

Despite his bid for the family trade and his efforts to entrench "polite vaudeville" in the manner of Cordray, Cort's Seattle Standard in the main followed current practice. This allowed the presence of women entertainers who could double as 'box rustlers' in the sale of liquor. The minor variety theatres round about were noisy and ill-kept. Public disapproval finally climaxed in city ordinances and the passage of the Barmaid Law.

Either by its quieter tone or by political pull, Cort's Standard escaped the storm. By 1890 he was at the peak of power, largely by sheer force of personality. Witty, handsome and a careful dresser, he was top man in the dramatic Donnybrook. But, cocky and aggressive, he tangled with the press, notably with redoubtable Colonel Blethen of *The Times,* for alleged slighting reviews of certain plays and players. Attempting to break his power, it is reported that the latter invited to the West magnates Klaw and Erlanger—a move soon to stir a hornet's nest.

Cort's Standard also furnished acts for the bucolic Leschi Pavilion out on Lake Washington. But with the opening of Cordray's new Third Avenue Theatre, which offered excellent stock plays—all liquor banned—the changing temper of the town quickly responded. Faced by business failure in the panic of '93, Cort relinquished major holdings, briefly leasing Paine's Opera House at Walla Walla, as anchor for his shrinking circuit, which still included Butte, Portland, and Spokane. In Chicago, as manager of its Imperial Theatre, he glumly awaited a turn of the tide.

This came, dramatically, with the Klondike gold rush of '97. Returning argonauts, pleasure bent, crowded Seattle's hotels, restaurants and, notably, its theatres, showering gold dust enroute. Property values sky-rocketed; mushroom theatres sprang up over night, some as short-lived. Back from far places came the managers: John Considine from Spokane, George Beede from San Francisco, and with great joy, from Chicago, John Cort, bursting with metropolitan ideas.

Scraping funds together, he rushed the building of the Palm

Garden, "a first class vaudeville house, on the plan of Koster and Beals of New York . . . no liquor allowed . . . Premises any Lady might visit with propriety." A roof garden was planned, but the building, for lack of funds, had to stop with the basement. The florid downstairs Palm Garden, planted in the heart of the town's business district at Cherry Street, drew civic protest. Normally, all such minor theatres were relegated to the flourishing skid road area beyond Yesler Way—the lumberjack's Valhalla. By reputed political influence, the Palm Garden kept its toehold, leaving lively legend of its stars: Cad Wilson, of Klondike fame, Gussie La More, friend of "Swiftwater Bill" Gates, and dozens more.

But though Cort countenanced burlesque, he also imported fine opera companies. At lush salaries, some played a full month, at low twenty-five cent tariff. Lavish as always, his public received full value. The golden tide of 1900 had also made possible the formation of the Pacific Amusement Company, with Cort as guiding spirit. He also completed his unfinished theatre, at a reputed cost of $40,000. Renamed the Grand Opera House, it was the city's finest theatre for many years. It likewise marked the fulfillment of a long-held dream: Cort's entrance into the legitimate field, to which he devoted the rest of his active life.

His daring and imagination now found wings. By option or lease, he gained control of many theatres along the westward route of the Northern Pacific Railway. When the far-off eastern magnates wakened at last to the West's latest Eldorado, they faced a formidable road block: Cort already owned most of the theatres. By hard necessity appointed their Northwestern agent, he was later to give them some bad moments.

The stage for Cort's entrance into the national scene was thus already set when nature and circumstance gave him the leading role. The Syndicate Rebellion, so-called, was no hasty upsurge. Thoughtful managers had long chafed under an absentee tight fist, though the earlier secession by Howe, Baker and others had been premature.

With the new century, however, flush days for the theatre had arrived. Business was brisk, the new czars hardheaded and sharp. The Seattle *Argus* of July 3, 1909 announced: "Next season Seattle will have eight large and completely equipped playhouses, each of the four managerial firms controlling two theatres: John Cort, the Moore and Grand; Russell and Drew, the Alhambra and Seattle; Considine, the Orpheum and Majestic; Pantages, the Lois and Pantages . . . This city now has as ample and diverse theatrical equipment as San Francisco." Be that as it may, West Coast lines were quite firmly drawn. Baker and Heilig, to the south, controlled an empire as large. All looked for a banner year—when a smouldering fuse suddenly ignited: the plays listed for their use were terrible.

Cort, off to New York for his 1910 bookings, found himself staring, in his own words, at an array of "dead ones." He also faced the short-tempered "Little Corporal" of the theatre, A. L. Erlanger. Curtly told that he could take what was given—or nothing—he retorted: "By George, that's a good idea. I think I'll take everything." Coolly picking up his hat, he departed. The war was on.

The "breezy Western diplomat," as the press dubbed him, soon had the Rialto buzzing with action. Western diplomacy, it was added, was "diplomacy with a big stick." Insurgents rose on every hand, the sympathetic Shuberts joined in, the disaffection spread wide. The basic idea of a central booking office for plays, to save time and confusion, was sound enough. But grave abuses had crept in, and percentages levied for mediocre plays were piratical. Actors as well as the public suffered from the squeeze.

With Cort as leader, the National Theatre Owners' Association was formed. It covered wide territory, adding to the substantial holdings of Calvin Heilig and Cort those of Moses Reiss in Ohio, Pennsylvania and West Virginia, as well as the major circuits in Texas and the South, in Illinois, Iowa, Nebraska and the Midwest. From ocean to ocean, upwards of 1,200 theatres were controlled. From within, it was aided by some of the nation's finest actors. Such independent spirits as Maude Adams, Minnie Maddern Fiske and her manager-husband had long battled the syndicates; so too had the inimitable Bernhardt earlier.

Cordray, Baker and other Northwest managers joined the fray with zest; Heilig began building "the most modern theatre west of Denver." In Seattle, managers Russell and Drew backed by the Shuberts, moved into the new Alhambra. The press of the day sizzled with innuendo and countercharge, but the final battle, furious though it had been, left a clearer horizon. Three full paid columns were needed to list syndicate offerings for the 1910 season: productions by Frohman, by A. H. Woods, a Ziegfeld creation, amid a blinding galaxy of stars . . . But where to put them? The local managers had the theatres.

Threats of massive building by the distant combine had failed to materialize. In Portland, a projected theatre at 13th and Morrison was never built. In Seattle, the neat Metropolitan duly rose, though never a financial success. In Spokane, the newly built American Music Hall was acquired by lease. With contracts on a long chain of theatres covering the entire region safely in pocket, topped by the modern Heilig, the challengers by compromise received the right to choose their billings. Syndicate offerings for the 1910 season were also billed in independent theatres. The freshman Northwest enjoyed its most brilliant season, and high noon in the nation's theatre was still to follow.

Cort, as manager of the expanding National Theatre Owners' Association, found his presence increasingly needed in their Broadway bookings. Disposing of his western interests in 1911, he returned to his native New York, thereafter to devote his time and energy to the legitimate theatre. The West was not forgotten. For the opening of his Cort Theatre there, he starred a former Seattle stock player, Laurette Taylor, in what proved a long run favorite—*Peg O' My Heart*. Cort's interests widened; he was at one time reputed to own more "high class theatres than any man in the world." Long before his death at his home in Scarsdale, New York, he had become a major figure of the American stage. He remains one of the Northwest's most able and energetic builders.

Storm and stress marked the changing fortunes of John Considine, burly lord of domain that far overflowed western bounds. He, like Cort, entered the theatre by its side door— variety; unlike the latter, his interest continued always with its more informal aspects. It was through Considine mainly that vaudeville, aided by timely impulses from its devotees, achieved a national sweep.

Arriving from Chicago just after Seattle's big fire of 1889, his Hibernian temperament found plenty of action as manager of its waterfront People's Theatre. He soon moved it "across the line" as had Cort, to less dubious quarters. Like other managers crippled by the financial depression of '93, Considine took temporary refuge in Spokane, "then rougher and tougher than Seattle." As manager of its main vaudeville theatre, he became involved in city and state ordinances forbidding the hiring of women entertainers where liquor was sold. Returning with the gold rush to Seattle, he retrieved from temporary managers the lease of the People's Theatre there.

To give his players wider scope, Considine, always a friend of popular entertainment, soon began building up a circuit to nearby towns. By 1906, as noted by Elliott in his lively *History of Variety-Vaudeville in Seattle,* Considine had established regular vaudeville houses in Spokane, North Yakima, Everett, Bellingham, Portland, Tacoma, Victoria and Vancouver—"the first legitimate popular-priced vaudeville chain in the world." Admission was ten cents. The idea spread rapidly; Considine soon stood next in the theatrical hierarchy to John Cort, with whom he had had an earlier business association at the People's Standard Theatre.

While visiting New York with friend Cort, Considine, a ready mixer, made a potent convert to his love of vaudeville in Timothy ("Big Tim") Sullivan, a Tammany chieftain. Sullivan furnished money and prestige; Considine stage experience and business ability. It was a congenial and long-lasting partnership.

On his return to the Northwest, Considine bought Cordray's Grand Theatre in Portland and built another $100,000 Grand in Tacoma, thus enlarging his Seattle holdings. Butte's Family Theatre was also added to his chain of handsome and expensive playhouses, soon to span the nation. The Star circuit, playing Portland, Tacoma, Seattle, Astoria and Vancouver was acquired in 1905. Moving out to the East, the International Theatre Company was organized, with headquarters in Chicago. A full year's booking was now possible, in twenty-one Northwest theatres and as many in California. The circuit ranged through Wisconsin, Michigan, Indiana, Pennsylvania, Ohio, Missouri, Kansas and Manitoba.

Vaudeville, strongly entrenched, attracted many gifted performers; with the decline of minstrelsy, it drew such scintillating blackface stars as George Primrose and Al Jolson. Though the popular ten and twenty-cent tariffs lingered, its artists received high salaries. This, multiplied by the number of acts, made production costly, and no doubt hastened its later retreat before the cheaper motion pictures. The fuzzy silent films, for a time used only to eke out the vaudeville acts, were soon to dominate them.

By 1908, vaudeville had become selective. It was now blazoned, in splashy ads, as "advanced," "refined," or "polite," in playhouses in all large cities. Reserved seats were 75 cents; there were season tickets. Eminent artists were booked at lush salaries, for two shows a day; short plays were featured, even experiments in grand opera. Tours could start from Broadway if desired; and for the West, Considine had large ideas. In Seattle, he leased the huge Coliseum built for a skating rink, turning it into a "block long theatre"—the largest west of Chicago. Seldom did theatres anywhere seat less than 1,800. Later, a fine new Orpheum was built at Seattle. In Portland, its largest playhouse, the revived Marquam Grand, served for a time as Considine's Orpheum as did the renamed Heilig, until a brandnew playhouse was built at Broadway and Main. Two sparkling circuits wove a bright web in the West, one ranging north from San Francisco, the other east from Denver. And those days the legitimate flourished as lushly, with the road shows at their zenith.

Expanding, the Sullivan-Considine circuit, now "the first transcontinental popular vaudeville in American history," affiliated with Orpheum circuits overseas. The best foreign acts were thus secured; taking the road from New York, seventy weeks' playing in major American cities was assured—Philadelphia, Washington, Pittsburgh, in theatres owned or leased by the firm. Their main office, however, remained in Seattle.

When partner Sullivan died in 1913, Considine sold his four million dollar holdings to eastern magnate Marcus Loew, of the

Orpheum franchise for the Northwest, and personally owned the theatres so named in both Seattle and Portland. He had accomplished enough for one man, and could view his work with later Keith-Loew circuit. Prosperous, he retained only his detachment.

No Horatio Alger was Considine's arch-rival, Alexander Pantages, though success for a time wrote a heady tale. A roving Greek emigrant who rose to dizzy heights, his life was filled with backstage intrigue, daring financial coups and blithe daily plottings for power and prestige.

A runaway sailor, Pantages edged into show business by way of the Alaskan honky-tonks, where he exhibited a genius for arranging dramatic programs. He crashed the scene farther south by opening, in 1904, the Crystal Theatre down on Seattle's seedy Second Avenue—a tiny "store show" with stage barely large enough for one entertainer or a trained animal act. Gold rush prosperity soon enabled him to "cross the line" to an uptown location at Seneca. Here, in a larger variety theatre named for its owner, Pantages put on better acts, mainly those billed on Considine's Star circuit. He also married a young violinist, whose name—Lois—adorned the very handsome theatre next built by him. This was to remain one of Seattle's most successful stock theatres until destroyed by fire in 1911.

His spectacular rise was perhaps due to his uncanny flair for guessing what his public wanted. A rover in many lands, he could speak several languages, though simple reading of English came hard. In building his early vaudeville chain to play Tacoma, Portland, Vancouver and Spokane, there was inevitable conflict with Considine, reigning czar of the two-a-day. Actors, animals or acrobats were daringly hi-jacked; contracts mysteriously cancelled—testifying as well to the zest of latter-day trouping.

By sharper practice or better showmanship, Pantages pushed his circuit southward. Six San Francisco theatres were bought at bargain rates after the fire; the Empire obtained from the Western Vaudeville Association. Purchase of the latter's Crystal circuit gave him the Rocky Mountain area also; soon after two Midwestern chains were added. He built a large theatre in Los Angeles, still in use, and by 1909 could assure players of most of a year's continuous billing. In Seattle, he built the handsome Pantages (1925) as his special stronghold. It remained in operation for fifteen years.

A born showman, Pantages enjoyed daring new acts, and keenly enjoyed catering to the public. A razor-sharp memory, a delight in battle and thorough knowledge of people aided in his rise. In business, he trusted no one, but was, however, much liked by helpers, to whom he was most generous. Circus folk all over the country called on 'Uncle Alex' in need. Wealth and luxury were savored by the former sailor. His home was palatial, his name flashed on marquees from coast to coast. Expanding also, he hired a European agent for scouting likely foreign acts. With lavish offices in Denver, San Francisco and New York, he still retained his head offices in Seattle, where he had made his start.

Pantages' later life was darkened by costly lawsuits—"frames for extortion," loyal associates protested—which consumed his fortune. Despite surface battles with Considine, the two men remained warm personal friends, bound by ties of common interest and marriage. It was to Considine that he sold out his theatre holdings, before illness and death in 1936 ended a highly dramatic career.

These are not all the men of action who built Northwest theatre. Other names rise readily: Russell and Drew, John Hanna, Keating and Flood, off-stage czars all. But these few, in linking it more closely to the larger American stage, created its more durable patterns. They will remain yesterday's dynasts.

The Storied / NINETIES

Many adjectives have been flung at the last years of the departed century: the gay, the naughty nineties, the waltzing nineties, the Mauve Decade. But to the theatre, they are much more than a caviar era, made fabulous by high living, Floradora girls and such colorful stage-door Johnnies as Diamond Jim Brady and his ilk. An opulent, high-stepping decade, its heady zest for living found outlet in epic spending. But its jingling pockets had been filled by epic deeds. Its playboys, under a thin veneer, turn out to be men of action. The times were larger than an adjective; its inner mood was sterner, harder. For the theatre, it was a day of splendor, of potent deeds, of stage immortals, still looming through nostalgic mists.

Mainly, its splendor lay in its great artists, now comfortably at home either in East or West. Illustrious stars, whose names revive strong magic: Bernhardt, the fading Booth, the rising George Arliss, the suave Drews, Irving and Terry, Salvini, Mansfield, and young Minnie Maddern Fiske. Assorted sirens for good measure: Lily Langtry, Mrs. Pat Campbell, Maxine Elliott, seductive Anna Held and a ripe bevy of beauties. A dedicated, lively crew, well fitted to adorn any stage.

Still unmatched for opulence are the playhouses built in that day. With today's stern accent on the functional still remote, builders flung in balconies and towers, elebrate grilles, Far Eastern minarets or Grecian pillars. Still somewhat awed by ancient patterns, the new world was dreaming up its own designs for living, not always suave or beautiful. The young Northwest, reaching for magnificence, had long forsaken frontier bareness.

Something of the glow of the times comes through in a quartet of playhouses just then rising. Largest by a shade was Portland's Marquam Grand, whose opening on February 10, 1890 by the Emma Juch Opera Company placed it squarely in the lap of the decade. Its most active life remains tied up with that period, though its full span covered some thirty-three years. Very checkered years, uneasy with their own drama.

Quite in keeping with the times was the announced intention of its builder, wealthy Judge A. P. Marquam, to build "the finest theatre on the Pacific Coast." Its chosen designer was J. M. Wood, reputedly "the foremost theatre architect of America." Though slightly smaller than San Francisco's famed Grand Opera House, also designed by Wood, the "beauty and completeness of exterior and interior finish and appointments" (so the proud local press reported), gave it top rating. It was designed for carriage trade.

For its plush opening, the local "400" turned out in jewels and furs; tickets had been auctioned at exorbitant prices; three carriage men directed the crowding traffic outside and looked after the proper calling of conveyances. Inside, guests dressed to the hilt crowded its handsome foyer, admiring its frescoed walls and lofty ceilings, its rich hangings of amber and blue velvet; its gleaming chandeliers, bronzes, marble columns and inviting lounge. The spacious auditorium seated 1,500 people, with capacity for standees; its elaborate star's dressing room was the largest of fifteen. There was an outsized property room, a fireproof scene room. Front page stories, enlivened by sketches, filled many columns; even the "chaste plumbing of the Ladies' and Gentlemen's Parlors" came in for praise, as displaying the most refined taste in furnishings and colorings. A framed picture of the garden scene from *Faust* adorned the ladies' room. Far cry indeed from drafty pioneer halls where oldtime troupers had launched their blood and thunder!

On stage, actors lacked no convenience. Its ample playing space, 42 x 70, and sixty feet high, was lighted by push button electricity, controlled by modern rheostat dimmer. Scenery was from Chicago; the spacious property room and scene room gave backstage comfort. Out front, rows of boxes, heavily curtained in velvet, flanked an elaborate proscenium. From here, patrons might view the stage, once the ornate curtain had lifted. This, following the current flair for foreign places, displayed a scene from Monaco, France. Below were stage boxes, a roomy orchestra pit and handsome opera chairs in circles: the effect was intimate, cosmopolitan. Prima donna Juch, responding to a tumultuous ovation, declared that "after visiting the finest theatres of this country and Europe [she] found this the equal of any," with "acoustic properties all that a singer could desire." A visiting stage manager pronounced the "hall, audience, decorations and music worthy of New York." Well, it had cost a cool $500,000! The Juch Company, opening in *Faust,* remained a full week. Later, a host of visiting artists, among them James A. Herne, who had opened the earlier New Market, returned in his own play, *Hearts of Oak.* So began the play-rich nights of a storied era.

The large building of which the theatre formed the core pre-empted a full half-block in the pulsing heart of the growing city's business district. The theatre was reached by a curved arch from the street, and was separated by solid fireproof brick walls from the office portion of the building. Across Morrison Street, and also facing Sixth, stood the fabulous Portland Hotel, "the most elegant caravansery in the Northwest," designed by Stanford White. Christened by a grand opening only a few weeks later, the hotel's unusual shape, its friendly verandas, gourmet cooking and corps of dusky waiters bore out the charm and color of its day. Globe-trotting presidents slept there; artists and assorted celebrities left tribute to its hospitality. Of the combination a local journal mused "that given an elegant, commodious hotel and a first-class theatre, you have the two most essential elements of a metropolis—the one catering to the physical wants of the genus homo; the other in large part giving to his mental faculties recreation and refreshment."

Cosmopolitan—that was the new and magic word! First lessee of the Marquam Grand was Al Hayman of San Francisco, later associated with Charles Frohman in New York. Soon, pockets comfortably filled with West Coast shekels, he was to shine on the Rialto. First resident manager was S. H. Friedlander; both were seasoned men of the theatre, in close touch with current tastes and trends. Head electrician was emerging tycoon George L. Baker. Able John P. Howe, who had suggested the building of the theatre, was shortly to leave for New York. Its completion spelled progress, in bold letters, for its host city.

It was not alone. Only slighty smaller than the Marquam Grand, and opening a month earlier, was the brand new Tacoma Theatre, also designed by Wood. Here the planner's imagination had run riot with an East Indian pagoda effect, carried out in eight proscenium boxes, vestibules, box office and elsewhere. Plenty of rich silk plush in the hangings; wainscoted walls, arches, bronzes, comfortable opera chairs with automatic backs and hat racks. Though the combined capacity of floor, balcony and galleries was somewhat less (1,200) than that of the Marquam Grand, the stage had the same full sweep, with two drop curtains, twenty-four complete sets of scenery, large dressing rooms, scene and property rooms, a handsome "box parlor," gentlemen's smoking lounge, plus "a multitude of other conveniences and appliances."

Unique in architecture, a gabled projection formed the theatre's main entrance. Stores filled out the street floor, with offices on its second and third stories. It was here that Calvin Heilig tried out his western wings. Tacoma, Washington, in the early nineties was enjoying an "excellent prosperity," as was the entire Puget Sound country, in a pre-depression boom. Keenest trade rival was its up-and-coming neighbor, Seattle, in a brisk duel matched only in vigor with that carried on with Portland to the south.

Tacoma's elegant playhouse was opened on January 13, 1890 by the Duff Opera Company, presenting the comic opera *Paola*. "In a city growing so rapidly and containing a large proportion of liberal and cultured people," declared the *West Shore*, "it will draw the finest histrionic talent in the United States, and will combine with Spokane Falls, Seattle and Portland . . . in forming a strong circuit for theatrical attractions." In charge was John Hanna, "a gentleman possessing wide experience as a manager," and one who played a major role in building up the Puget Sound theatrical circuit. The venture was highly successful to all concerned.

High-riding Spokane Falls, in eastern Washington, was by the nineties exchanging frontier brashness for more genteel manners. Gone were its noisy box houses; it jangly Gaiety Theatre, and the busy faro games of its salad days. Its crude Falls City Opera House had faded before a newer Grand, burned in '89. Here too city fathers, met in solemn conclave, decreed that a fine theatre was "good business" for the town. Funds promptly raised, into its building went civic hopes and dreams. Its splendor was to match that of the pace-setting Marquam Grand; within, the same spacious stage and working areas, the same lavish plush, of suitable hue. Its cost was somewhat less, but the new Grand Opera House—soon renamed the Auditorium Theatre—was rushed through in time for Spokane's Industrial Fair of 1890, now giving players welcome pause in the vast circuit embracing Idaho, Montana, Denver and Salt Lake City. The mines were humming; racy tales as to its *nouveaux riches* box-holders linger. Figures quoted by Grant in his *Story of Seattle's Early Theatres* show a rapid increase in the number of stage performances during the nineties, for all cities of the Northwest. Among these, Spokane's stage life stands out boldly.

Seattle, a husky giant of a town now climbing imperial hills, had almost forgotten its rag-tag past. But the raging fire that burned out its business district, almost on the verge of the era (1889), had also destroyed all of its theatres—Frye's fine opera house, John Cort's Standard and all. The only makeshift spared was Turner's Hall, built farther uptown for social and exhibition use by the Turn Verein. Though small, it had a usable stage and wings, and was at once pressed into service by manager Frye for presentation of road shows booked at his burned opera house. Frye's had seated 1,300. As the nineties dawned, Turner's was jointly leased by S. H. Friedlander of Portland's Marquam Grand and enterprising John Hanna of the Tacoma Theatre. It was completely remodelled; a larger stage built in, with new dressing rooms, curtains, scenery, opera chairs, frescoed walls and all the newest gadgets. Renamed the Seattle Theatre, it opened on September 13, 1890, starring Elsie Leslie in *The Prince and the Pauper,* with Fanny Warde and William Craig also in the cast.

A word of praise must here be recorded for the theatre's red-haired manager, John Hanna. Coming to Seattle shortly after the fire, he had successfully opened theatres at Tacoma and Olympia as well. Despite a badly equipped playhouse, he now won distinction for Seattle as an amusement center. Further, in a tilt with veteran schemer Al Hayman of San Francisco, he had, through "tact, sagacity and esteem" established on Puget Sound an independent circuit embracing fifteen cities. Throughout, the Sound cities displayed admirable spirit in the region's bid for dramatic independence, elsewhere described.

Hanna's regime at the makeshift Seattle lasted from September, 1890 to December of 1892. Under his aegis appeared such eminent stage folk as Thomas Keene in Shakespearean roles, Fanny Davenport in *Fedora* and *Tosca,* Louis James, Blanche Walsh, Lotta Crabtree in *Musette,* Maurice Barrymore, Emma Juch, Frank Daniels, Henrietta Crosman, May Robson, Sol Smith Russell, William Brady and others of stellar rank. But these days, all over the Northwest, its cities were running up handsome playhouses, bright symbols of civic growth. What of Seattle? The local press complained bitterly of "actors of worldwide reputation appearing in houses so poorly equipped." For Seattle, a town notable for expansive ideas, there could be but one answer. This came with the building of its brand new Seattle Theatre, fourth of a sumptuous quartet to grace the decade.

Its opening on December 3, 1892, declared the *Post-Intelligencer,* "marked a distinct step forward of this community in culture, intelligence and refinement." Underwritten by various public-spirited citizens, including J. D. Lowman, it was conveniently located at Third and Cherry. Flanked by the plush Rainier Club, its five-story structure rose proudly, its Italian Renaissance body adorned by a buff brick and chuckanut blue trim. Architect was Charles Saunders; its stage designer, Thomas Harrington of San Francisco. Its large stage, 40 x 70 x 62 feet, was equipped with all modern gadgets for scene shifting; more than $10,000 was spent for thirty complete sets of scenery painted by Thomas Moss of Chicago. There were thirteen dressing rooms and eight property rooms. The auditorium was done in modernized Louis XVI style with tiled floors and wainscoting; a novel stained glass window graced the foyer; sculptured heads of Tragedy and Comedy dominated the proscenium; the drop curtain showed a pleasure party returning from the Festival of Lights in Venice. Acoustics were superior. Costs of building, broadcast at $100,000, were designed to challenge the reigning Marquam Grand, though its seating capacity of 1,300 was slightly smaller.

A fine display of the exuberant Seattle spirit marked the premier. Tickets had been auctioned for fantastic sums, in tribute to popular John Hanna, who had outbid a Tacoma manager as its director. The cheapest box brought $175; Mr. Leigh Hunt, former owner of the *Post-Intelligencer,* paid $750 for his choice. Orchestra boxes went easily at $15, all proceeds above the regular two or three dollar tariff to be a gift to manager Hanna in tribute to his hustling. The Honorable John H. McGraw, governor of the state, made the dedication speech as the ornate curtain rose on the J. C. Duff Opera Company's presentation of a double bill: *A Trip to Africa* and *Cavalleria Rusticana.* Hanna, remaining in charge until 1895, was succeeded for a time by Calvin Heilig. In 1898, John P. Howe was called from New York to preside over its fortunes, there to continue until his withdrawal from the theatre in 1905. As Seattle's major legitimate theatre, the new playhouse functioned until 1915, when the present Arctic Club was built on its site.

With its four major cities now equipped with handsome theatres, the Northwest enjoyed the nation's finest artists. Julia Marlowe appeared in *Much Ado About Nothing;* Frederick Warde and Louis James in *Julius Caesar,* with the Barrett settings; E. H. Sothern in *Captain Letterblair;* Richard Mansfield in *Beau Brummel;* Blanche Walsh in *Aristocracy;* Henry Irving and Ellen Terry with the London Lyceum Company in *The Merchant of Venice;* the Drew Comedy Company with Mrs. John Drew, Mrs. Sidney Drew and Lionel Barrymore in *The Rivals;* Fanny Davenport in *Cleopatra* and *La Tosca;* Thomas Keene in *Hamlet, Louis XI* and *Richard III;* Kyrle Bellew and Mrs. Brown Potter in *Society* and *Camille;* William Gillette in *Too Much Johnson;* the William Brady production of *Trilby.* The illustrious host numbered also Maxine Elliott, Nat Goodwin, Robert Mantell, Maurice Barrymore, William Faversham and Mary Hampton, Patti Rosa and others.

The taste of the day ran the gamut. Effie Essler gladly returned in her *Hazel Kirke,* to wipe out memories of the cruel fire. Comedy played the field, offering Eddie Foy in *The Strange Adventures of Miss Brown;* Frank Daniels in *Little Puck;* Lottie Collins rocked the rafters in her hit song, "Ta-Ra-Ra-Boom-de-ay." Melodrama lurked darkly: in a current sensation, *The Span of Life,* three acrobats formed a living bridge, with the shuddering heroine and her babe crossing the deep chasm on their bare backs. Not yet had the new century reaction from stark realism to the stripped symbol set in.

Out in the larger world, certain local players had found the spotlight: Blanche Bates, Laurette Taylor, Nance O'Neill, Margaret Illington of Tacoma later. At home, Ida Gaskell, actress wife of John Cort, occasionally appeared on stage. Out in rural La Grande, Oregon, Maude Durbin, future wife and leading lady for Otis Skinner, was shyly beginning a stage career by giving readings or arranging dramatic programs, during a winter spent with parents there.

The West was in retreat. Out in cattle country, at Pendleton, it was not too long since Frederick Warde, playing *Virginius,* had been startled—and pleased—by the guttural acclaim, in his high moments, of local gallery gods—a row of blanketed Umatillas. Ten gallon hats were still standard there, but there were many, many more good plays.

But players now sometimes sought the West where it had long fled. At metropolitan Seattle, busily pushing the 50,000 mark, the romantic Bernhardt, determined on a bear hunt, proudly "shot" a huge stuffed *Ursa* obligingly placed in a convenient thicket by an amused Chamber of Commerce. The tanned hide with its deadly bullet holes was a treasured possession of the diva, along with the rosewood coffin she always carried on tour. The tall tree country had never lacked a sense of humor. Nor had the divine Sarah in any way lost her magic, playing to packed houses along the way. A buoyant sense of well-being, barely nicked by a transient depression, and not yet chilled by a world war, everywhere animated both actors and audience.

Theatres were lost as well as found in the nineties. The Dalles, Oregon, had built three of them. It had been commended for the $10,000 spent in service of the arts when its first one rose in '84—the town itself described in the *West Shore* as "the most solidly built town in the state outside of Portland" at the time. The second, placed uptown at Third and Washington four years later, had been larger and finer. Wiped out by fire, Maximilian Vogt, whose general store carried everything from a needle to a tractor, had replaced it with one vying with the best in Portland.

All was modern—ample stage and working areas, with plenty of plush out front. When the town itself was later partly razed, the theatre's handsome interior was gutted, though the walls still stood. Vogt, discouraged, did not build for a time.

During an uneasy interim in the early nineties, players here took refuge in two smaller halls—Wingate's and Baldwin's. But in 1894, Vogt, aided by funds loaned by German friends ($50,000), replaced the roof of his opera house, building in a much larger stage and inclined floor. Its appointments were also suitably handsome. Part of the sturdy three-story structure was rented as an armory, and for offices. The rebuilt Vogt Opera House sheltered all major road shows during the latter nineties and later. It was not until the new century (1911) that fire again struck, this time leaving only the bare walls. And this time the theatre was not rebuilt. River traffic had slackened somewhat. Though a corner of the impressive ruin is still used as a garage, plays are now staged in a neat high school auditorium.

Fire also plagued Astoria. Here the spacious Ross Opera House, built by enterprising citizens in the mid-eighties, held over as the town's major theatre. Prima donna Juch delighted an overflow crowd of 2,000 there in the nineties, and its playbills list the most distinguished artists of the day: Otis Skinner, James A. Herne, Emma Abbott, Margaret Mather and Frederick Warde among them.

Like the region itself—and the town—Ross' Opera House had a dual nature. Movable platforms made it possible to stage more rugged entertainment for its skid road patrons — greased pig contests, prize fights. It was crowded to the aisles when John L. Sullivan fought here, even going down in folk-song as "the fishing village of Astoria where John L. Sullivan fought." Minstrels were much liked: Billy Emerson did almost as well when he appeared. Melodrama lingered. Friendly and versatile, well liked by the town, the playhouse was remodelled after long service. When razed by fire, about 1892, it was not rebuilt.

Instead, farther uptown, the more modern Fisher's Opera House rose at 15th and Exchange, to breast the fortunes of the new century. From 1902 on, practically all major travelling companies played here. Though decked out with fancy opera chairs and brand new stage gadgets, oldtimers for some reason cling to memories of the older Ross Opera House. But Fisher's lived out two minor fires, until destroyed by the holocaust which made a disaster area of the town in 1922. Though only a few blocks of its business district were left standing, strangely spared was a corner of the town's first theatre down by the riverfront.

Some minor theatres kept things lively in the nineties. Billed at its Theatre Comique, some of its variety stars were a high-stepping lot. Cad Wilson, parading in her carriage in Paris gowns and frilly parasol, caused as much excitement off-stage as did Seattle's gold rush favorites. But for that matter, many of the ladies came from there.

Life in the Oregon Country moved with the urgent sweep of the larger current outside—at times with more untamed vigor. Though sawmills, shipyards and steamboats agitated the coast country, show folk still found travel difficult, the playhouses few and small. When the Odd Fellows put up a fair-sized solid brick hall at Marshfield in 1889, its roomy stage and auditorium were a boon to players through the nineties. Mainly these were the smaller regional stock companies, among whom the Margaret Iles Company and the Margretta Fischer troupe were high favorites. The New Market Company came down from Portland in 1884, presenting *Rosedale, or The Rifle Ball*. Local thespians put on make-up, but it was not until 1900 that the larger Masonic Hall gave the drama a needed lift. Home of many a rousing melodrama, it survives as the Blue Mouse Theatre, now pre-empted by movies. Both these early theatres hugged the waterfront. The more modern high school auditorium which replaced them sought the nearby hills.

In the smaller towns, the so-called opera houses were quite often built by either the Masonic or Odd Fellows lodges, doubling valiantly as community centers. At inland Myrtle Point, its three-story brick Odd Fellows Hall, built in 1892, was host to various touring companies. Roseburg, still farther inland, built its brick opera house (Odd Fellows Hall) in 1890. Though somewhat off-center for major companies, stray troupes occasionally stopped. Far down the coast, Crescent City and Bandon had long had makeshift community halls.

The valley towns in general reserved their building till the new century. At Eugene, a favorite overnight stop between San Francisco and Portland, the nineties witnessed a full quota of entertainment in drafty upstairs Rhinehart's Theatre, later called Parker's Opera House. Listed are the Tittell Sisters in *M'liss* and *Frou-Frou;* Richard French in *Dr. Jekyll and Mr. Hyde;* the able Frawley Dramatic Company; popular Katie Putnam; the Calhoun Opera Company in *The Black Hussar* and many others. Mr. Frohman, after "400 nights in New York" presented *Jane.* Robert Ingersoll and Bill Nye lectured; Joaquin Miller's play *The Danites* was given in his home town by the Stutz Company in November of '94—the poet himself just then in the Sandwich Islands. Louis James, scheduled to play *Spartacus* at the University's Villard Hall, was obliged to substitute *My Lord and Some Ladies* for lack of backstage room. The town's lively thespians, coached by visiting professional Catherine Cogswell (Thorne) put on a series of favorite plays, including those of Shakespeare and Sheridan, spiced by several light operas. The fine brick Opera House which rose in 1903 stressed new century prosperity.

Neighboring Corvallis, site of the state's agricultural college, worried along with a veteran playhouse built before the '80s as a Masonic Hall and courthouse, though a Portland company spurned its shelter. Needled by the press, the theatre, currently known as the Majestic, received several remodellings. It carried on until far down in the present century, with modern assists. When torn down in 1950 it had long lapsed to mercantile use. Meanwhile the town's brilliant Maude Hoffman in the '90s was receiving acclaim in this country and abroad as leading lady for Wilson Barrett, portraying Ophelia and other demanding roles.

Albany's makeshift playhouse often received absent treatment from the larger touring companies, though visited by regional stock companies and stray minstrels until burned in 1898. The Hamlin's Wizard Oil shows made annual rounds hereabouts; the tent repsters later filled an aching gap with Pete-and-Toby shows and rural drama. And, by recompense, Albany was a major strong-hold of the Chautauqua movement for the upper valley.

The state's capital, Salem, greeted the gay nineties with a neat new playhouse, the Grand, to replace aging Reed's Opera House.

Though built by the Odd Fellows, with an upstairs lodge room, its first floor theatre was modern and pleasing. Actors found its well-lighted stage and roomy working areas a vast improvement. Patrons enjoyed its comfortable folding chairs, plush hangings and fresh decor. Leased by John Cordray, its playbills list an impressive array of stars during the decade. The Salem Grand, as earlier mentioned, was retained by Cordray for the Legitimate for years after he had sold his Portland theatre to the Keith vaudeville circuit. The town early organized a robust and flourishing Drama League which sponsored both road and home productions. Fire and flood here somehow stayed their hand, and the Grand, long housing road shows, is currently in active use for motion pictures. The nineties just missed the nostalgic closing of Reed's on April 20, 1900 with Barlow's Minstrels, for which practically the whole town turned out. Also the triumphant premiere at the Grand in December of the same year of the Grau Opera Company in *The Little Tycoon, El Capitan* and *The Chimes of Normandy*.

Hustling neighbors had overshadowed mellow Oregon City, to the north. Shively's Opera House, its wooden playhouse of the decade, strange in architecture, offered more space but little comfort, in replacing older Pope's Hall. There was a good-sized stage, with wings and drop curtain. Its echoing auditorium, reached by broad outdoor stairs, was lighted by an ornate gas chandelier. The wooden seats were hard, the dressing rooms tiny and dark, but the smaller touring road shows plastered its backstage areas with posters and playbills of current dramas. Shively's ran down into the new century, its downstairs store crammed with antiques guarded by its owner, Miss Lillean Shively. When the ungainly building at last succumbed to wreckers in 1954, a bygone era was in retreat. Here too fire and flood had been merciful, and the town's pioneer brick opera house, Pope's, still does part-time mercantile service. As the nineties faded, the town's dramatic taste was slaked by Chautauqua plays. Gladstone, on its outskirts, was the state's major fortress. And there was Portland, with its several theatres, but a few miles distant.

How swiftly the railroads changed the map! Jacksonville, bypassed in their route, settled into the shadows. Nearby Medford, girt by lush orchards, was briskly running up its Page and later

/157

Wilson Opera House for passing road shows. Ashland, on the Southern Pacific's upward climb, built its Gagniard Opera House as the decade bowed in, as more fitting to its entertainers. This they duly noted. The Lithia Theatre built in 1913 across from a large hotel of that name, marked the town's emergence as a health resort, by virtue of its mineral springs. Later christened the Vining Theatre, for a time it sheltered an active resident repertory company until razed by fire in 1954.

Out in the sagebrush reaches, Baker City was to lose its standby Rust's Opera House. Even before the railroads came in '84, the *Daily Sagebrush* had lauded Joseph Jefferson, Nellie Boyd, James O'Neill and many others appearing in the "old wooden opera house." Troupers mainly favored the quick approach offered by the pioneer Utah, Idaho and Oregon stage route established in the '50s, which led out to Montana and beyond. Some used the longer river route from Portland, up through The Dalles.

Whichever way they came, they were welcome, in a town noted for boom-or-bust psychology. In one upsurge, President Harrison visited the town in 1891, arriving by rail from Portland with a party of 300. Baker, as it was now called, did not share in the general depression of '93; on the contrary, while Portland endured panic, times there remained lively, due to rich mining strikes nearby. Despite the heavy winter of '97, with its snow and floods, many of the town's main structures were then erected. Later, alleging "unfair action" of the Chase National Bank, the local bank closed its doors. A fire which destroyed several frame buildings the following year, razed Rust's faithful opera house. Its builder, older and tired by then, did not replace it. Instead, energetic citizens of the town, many of them people of wealth and culture, realizing its civic value, raised the necessary funds for a new and handsome one.

The new Baker Theatre, phoenix of the passing nineties, was ambitious indeed. No downstairs stores here tolerated. Instead, a full gallery and plenty of plush. It was here that emerging tycoon George Baker singed youthful wings as the new century dawned. Its later playbills list such fine artists as Viola Allen, George

Broadhurst in *Bought and Paid For* and *The Lottery Man;* the Brandon Opera Company for a full week (1925), presenting such favorites as *The Chocolate Soldier, Robin Hood, The Bohemian Girl* and *Chimes of Normandy.* The inland metropolis also enjoyed "fashionable vaudeville" and minstrels.

No such fine fare heartened the little towns, shut off by bad roads. Homemade plays, stray third-class road shows, circuses or medicine shows were their lot. But even in the cities, tastes differed sharply: it was that old cleavage between drifters and stayers. The nineties even seemed to deepen the region's split personality. Cities had their torrid skid roads, their cool Nob Hills. Portland's carriage trade flocked to the Marquam Grand for opera, at fancy prices. Nothing could have been more boring to the loggers, swaying along Burnside Street to Erickson's mile-long bar. A good rousing burlesque show for them.

So too at Seattle. Its handsome new Seattle Opera House, built early in the decade, paced the durable Third Avenue, successor to Cordray's second Musee'. Both were strongholds of the Legitimate, throughout the '90s and later. Down near the line, Cort's New Standard Theatre, mainly variety, had revived with a bang in the Klondike gold rush of '97. A dozen store shows and music halls lurked roundabout: the Bella Union, Ranke's Hall and others featured burlesque or variety.

Fully in tune with its day was a theatre which ushered in the nineties at Olympia, Washington. Opening on December 26, 1890 with suitable fanfare, it reflected as well the yeasty spirit of its builder, John Miller Murphy, editor of the *Washington Standard* and earlier newssheets. An avid lover of good plays, it was largely through his efforts that a proper theatre rose. Crowned by a squat square tower, the Olympic's architecture was far from beautiful, but within, its furnishings reflected the lavish spirit of the times. Its sleek plush hangings, elaborately fringed, its exotic painted drop curtain and roomy backstage areas evoked purple passages from the press. Patrons were enchanted. Its first-night offering, *Little Lord Fauntleroy,* under the Hayman aegis, was a social and civic event. Minnie Radcliffe starred as Lady Errol; in days to come Lotta Crabtree played there in *Musette.* Mainly through

Murphy's tireless energy, major artists of the day faced its footlights for a full twenty years. The old playhouse withstood progress until 1925.

Stage folk were always warmly welcomed in another good show town, Walla Walla, in the wheat country beyond. Its Gaiety Theatre, opened in '79, had been one of the first in the territory. Replaced by Small's ambitious opera house in 1884, eastern road shows and resident stock companies had gladly stopped there. Playhouses blossomed in the smaller towns. Inland Centralia built a new opera house early in 1890; Yakima, in the fruit belt, declared its plush opera house "one of the finest in the Northwest." Far up on the Sound, younger sawmill towns, Bellingham and Everett, ran up theatres of sorts. Historic Port Townsend, classic example of frontier boom or bust, had edged out its venerable Masonic Hall, built in 1855, by much larger Learned's Opera House in 1884. But its boom was fading.

Unique on several counts was an opera house which rose in the early nineties far up in the timbered Olympic Peninsula. Port Angeles, Washington—the only townsite in the nation except for Washington, D. C. established by presidential decree—had been set aside by Lincoln as a naval reserve because of its magnificent harbor. But it had other claims to a storied past. There had migrated in the fading '80s a group of hopeful settlers bent on founding a model commonwealth, or cooperative colony, along lines inspired by Robert Owen and by French social reformers. Drawing both eager dreamers and hard-headed farmers, the colony from the start had fostered both drama and debate. Even in its first sprawling community center, Potlatch Hall, down at the East End, a play had been put on by amateurs, coached by a professional actor who had directed at the Liberal Club of Birmingham, England. Its walls throbbed with action, the town just then stirred by real estate, coal and railroad booms. For its opening, Emma Thursby, "reigning queen of the concert stage" was billed.

Though the diva by some mischance failed to appear, boom days drew in many stray troupers: the McKee-Rankin Company from San Francisco in a series of plays, with Nance O'Neill turning in her first lead role in *The Danites;* Sol Smith Russell in *Edge-water Folks;* Jessie Shirley in *The Lady of Lyons* and current dramas. Local players with their British coach staged *The Ticket of Leave Man, Meg's Diversion, The Spy of Atlanta.* There were grand masquerade balls, under flickering kerosene lights; the fashionable "German" was danced there; political orations were hot and impassioned; commencement speeches droned on. *The Chimes of Normandy, The Mikado* were given by local singers; a lively minstrel show. Long after the demise of the colony, the old opera house, beating heart of the town's social life, gamely staved off progress for a full thirty years.

Many a frontier town, on both sides of the Columbia and far out in the mountain country, under a new and more genteel front, cherished memories of a rake-hell past—or of far more lively days. Center of it all would be its aging opera house, where time had somehow paused in its mad flight, leaving strong magic. The nineties offered much more splendid playhouses, though not always more chills or thrills. Out in the more rugged mountain country, Idaho City's old Temple Theatre (later the Jenny Lind) as it gave way to plush and gilt, could have furnished many such. So too Silver City, where Charlotte Crampton had played. In Montana, Butte's new opera house was fully in the modern ornate mood, as was that at Great Falls. There were many such, just now seldom dark as the road shows whizzed through. Stock companies were active, too. The busy towns, outliving both boom and bust, scarcely stopped to consider that they might be leaving their youth behind.

And in all the bustle and building, the players still reigned supreme; the Legitimate enjoyed top billing . . . The nineties faded out in warm, rich glow. Stirring days were yet to come.

NEW CENTURY / *on Stage*

The present century, later haggard with change, swept out from the wings with poised assurance. So also did the stars. For the theatre, it was to be its finest hour. Special cars, champagne, jewels rewarded the most successful; the buxom stage sirens basked in golden plenty. Blond Lillian Russell of Iowa accepted from good friend Diamond Jim Brady, as a small token of admiration, a gold-plated bicycle, its mother-of-pearl handlebars studded with rubies, emeralds and—naturally—diamonds. But in all this cheerful affluence, it was not Beauty alone who took toll. It was the day of the thespian, from tattered buskin up.

And by no means the home-grown product solely. The cult for foreign artists was devout. Bernhardt's famous ten farewells to America were played out in the fervid atmosphere of exotic food, silk-lined dressing rooms, and priceless jewels then deemed native to the foreign diva. Eager fans stood all night in line for even a brief glimpse of the rare being. The foreign opera star could demand—and get—fabulous sums for a single appearance. Patti's usual modicum was $5,000; her yearly salary, as assured by older Europe's royal munificence, reputedly well beyond $50,000. American songbirds, by thrifty change of name, could do almost as well; actors for some reason stubbornly clung to their own monikers. But though blond Lillian's favorite food continued to be quoted—perhaps significantly as "corn on the cob"—her collection of Chinese porcelains was likewise notable. A fine stir of aspiration quickened the air.

In all this new century effulgence, one must not overlook the muscular stamina of the stage of that day. American actors had won respectful attention abroad, among them Edwin Booth, in tragic roles; folksy Joseph Jefferson, prima donna Emma Abbott: the number was to grow with the years. At home, a spirited young crew was crowding into the footlights: Minnie Maddern Fiske, James K. Hackett, the suave Sothern, the Drew-Barrymore family, Richard Mansfield, Maude Adams, to name but a few of those who were to become household names, known from coast to coast.

Playgoing was a national habit, firmly entrenched. In the early twentieth century, New York with her forty-nine operating theatres edged out beyond such mellow old-world capitals as London, listing thirty-nine, or Paris with twenty-four. Broadway blazed with famous names, almost as well known in Kalamazoo and Walla Walla. But as the frontier faded, the theatre itself had become more complex. New patterns were on stage. Liveliest of these was a buxom charmer nourished by the prosperous nineties—musical comedy. As far back as 1866, at Niblo's Garden in New York, a costly, eye-snatching production called *The Black Crook* had racked up 474 performances in its initial engagement. Ladies cavorting in pink tights had set tongues wagging, but the triple assault of music, the dance and spectacle had been deadly. In the years between, an engaging crew of near-relatives had stormed on stage: extravaganzas, pantomimes, variety acts, minstrel shows, revues. The family was immense. In 1903, twenty-five percent of all Broadway productions had been musicals. The number did not lessen with the years.

The better music halls, Weber and Fields or Tony Pastor's, had launched such formidable stage figures as Lillian Russell and David Warfield. Their programs were reviewed along with those of the Legitimate; the more clever burlesques ranked as important shows of the year. Spectacle became increasingly important in the lush Ziegfeld Follies of the fertile '20s and the later George White Scandals, which toured extensively. A scanty plot was here amply rounded out in music, dance and lavish costume. The tempo of the times was increasing; size and numbers becoming important in the reach for the bigger and better. By the magic of technicians, the stage vibrated with color and movement.

Add also light opera: *The Merry Widow, The Student Prince, Blossom Time* and a score of others, each with its galaxy of stars. And each edging out to new playing records—a year, two years, three, down to the crashing climax of today's *Oklahoma!* and *South Pacific*. Though Gilbert and Sullivan remained stand-bys, opera began a wistful search for native themes, fully realized in *Porgy and Bess.*

But the legitimate stage was breaking records too. Otis Skinner by popular demand was held in his marathon role in *Kismet* for four full years. *Tobacco Road, Life with Father* stretched out endlessly, scarcely moving from their Broadway stance. The play, the player and the technician had found new accord. The stage designer no longer hauled locomotives, swinging bridges, chariots on stage for thrills; melodrama was pretty much 'old hat.' For the newer decor, a few bold lines, masses of light or color suggested palace or hovel, penthouse or factory; the electrician too had discovered new worlds. More important, the actor now brooded more on inner meaning than on pompous gesture. With the new century, the American stage was reaching for maturity.

What was the role of the Pacific Northwest in all this vivid scene? Yesterday it had been to furnish swelling audiences for scarce playhouses. The westward push had by no means stopped. Neither migrant nor oldtimer had lost his eager love of theatre. San Francisco, Denver, Salt Lake City were banner theatre towns; the Oregon Country had been stage-struck from the start. There was a pleasant jingle of shekels out there . . . The tycoons were attentive.

Portland's Heilig, already described, was the answer to a challenge. At Seattle, magnates Cort, Russell and Drew, Considine and Pantages ruled at eight assorted theatres. Tacoma already had its ornate opera house designed by Wood; the bright new Savoy opened in May, 1907. Spokane had run up its commodious Auditorium Theatre on a scale to satisfy the show-loving town. Many smaller Washington towns kept in the running with less pretentious playhouses.

In Oregon, modern theatres greeted the century at Salem, Astoria and Baker City. Eugene announced prosperity with a brick opera house, opened in 1903. Medford replaced older playhouses with its Medford and Page opera houses, successively; Ashland's Lithia Theatre (later the Vining) rose in 1913. In Portland, the Columbia was built in 1904, anticipating a fair, the Heilig and New Baker later. All did flourishing business, down through the twenties. Ornate theatres pegged important cities of Idaho and Montana; to the north, Victoria's ample opera house had long been a magnet for troupers. As the century dawned, the pleased attention always given the stage in the Oregon Country burst into ardent flame. Its spirited rejection of shoddy plays had been fully in character.

Bookings for these new theatres, reaching from British Columbia down through the Rocky Mountain and Sound areas to California and farther, were now made in John Cort's New York office, from there channeled outward to various parts of the country by the larger National Theatre Owners' Association.

But though the battle had been fought—and won—by theatres, most plays were still controlled by the distant syndicates. Listed for 1910 were productions by Frohman, Belasco, Cohan and Harris and such stellar managers. Pledged artists were John Drew, Wm. H. Crane, Otis Skinner, David Warfield, Blanche Bates, Ethel Barrymore, Sarah Bernhardt (in a repertory of nineteen plays), Maude Adams, Nance O'Neill, Lillian Russell, Blanche Walsh, amid a shining host. Two companies from the London Gaiety Theatre were abroad; Ziegfeld presented Anna Held. *Ben Hur* was going strong; so too were *The Merry Widow, The Fortune Hunter* and *Chauncey Olcott*. Now, by the hard-won open door policy achieved by compromise with eastern czars, the Northwest swung strongly out into the larger current of the times. Outside, President Taft was just then praising the theatre as "restful" and "to be commended for holding a mirror up to nature."

How swiftly now change laid rude hands on the structure of the theatre! It was in the troubled twenties, torn by post-war disillusion, that the American playwright found his voice. Earlier, trying out native themes, the homely realism of James A. Herne had made the facile melodramas of Boucicault seem empty and outworn, even the sleek Bronson Howard comedies somewhat affected. Herne's somber *Margaret Fleming,* praised by realist William Dean Howells, his homely *Hearts of Oak* and later *Sag Harbor,* had struck a deeper chord. William Vaughan Moody was soon to cross the Mississippi with his *Great Divide;* Belasco's *Girl of the Golden West* to provide nostalgic theme for a Puccini opera, done at the Metropolitan. The rakish western cowboy was yet to ride onstage in Lynn Riggs' *Green Grow the Lilacs,* later stuff for the fabulous musical, *Oklahoma!* But writer Paul Green was searching the deep South for his *No 'Count Boy, In Abraham's Bosom, The House of Connolly.* All this literary searching was not without potent cause. In the fertile twenties, Director Drummond of Cornell's drama classes, Koch at North Carolina, Arvold in North Dakota were sending forth both writers and players bent on portraying their region just as it was, with truth and clarity. Notably, the impulse had been nurtured by the more sophisticated George Pierce Baker of Harvard and Yale. Critical but kindly, he had managed to foster a dream of The Great American Play.

Dark-browed Eugene O'Neill, seeking the universal, had reached backward to Greek tragedy; Maxwell Anderson pulled out the reedy stops of blank verse. Outlets for these exploring craftsmen were certain congenial acting groups: the Provincetown, the Washington Square Players, the Neighborhood Playhouse, working thriftily off Broadway. In the '30s the urban Group Theatre became socially conscious in the persons of playwrights Elmer Rice, Clifford Odets and others, meanwhile training many able players for the stage. The forthright modern Naturalism outdated the neat drawing room comedies of Clyde Fitch, amusing though they might be. Also, the struggling acting groups left progeny: Manhattan's brilliant Theatre Guild derives directly from the Washington Square. Later heirs were to be many ardent university acting groups and the emerging "little theatres" of the nation. Out in the Northwest, as elsewhere, change plowed deep, with native roots putting forth fresh branches. New dramatic patterns were in the making, a few worth a passing word.

Torchbearer for avant garde experiment in the Sound country was Seattle's Cornish School of Music and Drama, known far beyond the region as champion of the contemporary in the arts. Its founder, Miss Nellie Cornish, as far back as 1914, had presented in an upstairs recital room leading exponents of the modern dance, of expressionistic drama, of new-style music, haled from Austria, Paris or Berlin. Modest beginnings were soon outgrown, and, underwritten by citizens and outsiders, the Cornish Foundation was established, by coincidence in the same year as New

166/

York's pioneering Washington Square Players. Retained as life-long director of its board of trustees was yeasty "Miss Nellie," devotee of the fusion of the arts. The spacious Moorish-type building erected on Capitol Hill to serve its expanding needs was for many years an artistic and social center for much of the Northwest.

Its theatre, seating 300, was during the twenties an arena for experiment in drama. Chosen as co-directors, fresh from Chicago's trail-blazing Little Theatre, were esthete Maurice Browne and his actress-wife, Ellen Van Volkenberg. Just completed was a nation-wide tour in the first American production of Gilbert Murray's translation of *The Trojan Women*. Browne, an exponent of the art theatre movement, later achieved fame for the London production of his play, *Wings Over Europe*. Ellen Van Volkenberg, gifted actress and skilled director, for some years delighted playgoers, meanwhile influencing their tastes.

The Brownes, billed in 1920 for an eighteen-week season, formed their so-called Art Repertory Theatre, made up of capable players recruited from Broadway and elsewhere, with some local professionals. Prominent among these was Moroni Olson, recent support for Margaret Anglin in her Broadway appearance in *The Trial of Jeanne d'Arc*. With experiment strongly to the fore, this first season produced the American premiere of Claudel's *The Tidings Brought to Mary* and of Arthur Davison Ficke's *Mister Faustus*. Original plays—particularly by American writers —were sought, and poetic drama was favored. Among the players were Byron Foulger, a future director of Portland's Civic Theatre, and his wife, Dorothy Adams, together with Oregon-born Janet Young, later known to Broadway.

The Cornish, as it was familiarly called, soon offered training in stage design, languages, eurythmics, fencing, to round out its main courses in music and the dance. At its peak, a staff of forty-five trained experts guided some 150 selected students from all over the country. On Browne's departure for Europe in the early '20s, Ellen Van Volkenberg assumed directorship, not only teaching the dramatic arts but playing leads in major productions. At nearby Tacoma, a town strongly theatre-conscious and active in the fledgling drama league movement, she directed a summer session which featured a revival of *The Trojan Women*. A pioneer in the art of puppetry, an early group trained by her toured the West Coast extensively. At the Cornish, famous for its hospitality, a long list of artists either taught or were entertained on tour. Among these were singers Gadski, Matzenauer; dancers Pavlova and the Denishawn group; musicians Rudolf Ganz, Spalding, members of the Flonzaley Quartet, drama critic Clayton Hamilton, from a shining aggregation.

Up from California for the summer of 1922 came pundit Sam Hume, presenting plays of a lighter type: Wilde's *Importance of Being Earnest,* and *Tea for Three.* He was succeeded as co-directors by Mr. and Mrs. Burton James, late of New York's Neighborhood Playhouse. The plays at this time became more socially conscious, but sprinkled among C. S. Brooks' *Wapping Wharf* or Dreiser's *Laughing Gas* were plays by Shaw, Galsworthy, Barrie and Dickens. The gay *Cornish Follies,* stressing the allied arts of music, dance and drama, were presented with interesting stage design.

Mr. and Mrs. James later founded their own Civic Repertory Playhouse, built on the edge of the Washington campus. An ambitious production of *Peer Gynt,* with incidental music, drew a wide audience from the Northwest. Continuing the strong slant toward experiment, the work of local playwrights was presented. During the post-war days of the later '20s and '30s the pair were active in W.P.A. theatre and the Washington Educational Theatre. Following a major shift of personnel, the University of Washington School of Drama acquired the playhouse, currently used as one of its four active theatres.

Direct offshoot of the Cornish School were the Moroni Olson Players—the Northwest's "pioneer circuit repertory company." Their range, however, spread out over Rocky Mountain territory as well. Operating from a base in Ogden, Utah, their circuit during the late twenties played in some twenty-five Northwestern cities. Their founder and organizer, whose name the group bore, was joined by eight professionals from as far east as Maine and as far west as Vancouver, B. C. Their aim: to provide the region with "distinctive drama," in other words, with somewhat better plays than the commercial theatre might provide. Most active aides of the director were Byron Foulger and his wife, Dorothy Adams, with Oregon-born Janet Young. At a time when road shows were becoming scarce, these players added acceptably to the current dramatic fare. Several of them later joined the motion picture colony.

Older Portland, meanwhile, well furnished with good plays by its competent Baker Stock Company, had not strayed too far from the conventional. Practically all major road shows were well mounted at its handsome Heilig, which also billed singers, dancers, musical comedies or what not. Baker himself had always been noted for experiment. When he withdrew in 1915, the theatre itself was in transition. The later movements of his group have been noted. A newer stock company, the Forrest Taylor Players, became prominent as the twenties wore on; they were succeeded about 1925 by the highly popular Duffy Stock Company, which had its own playhouse, the Dufwin. Such engaging players as Jane Darwell, Leo Carillo, Marie Dressler, rotating among the major coast cities, had a loyal following, and played well down into the mid-thirties.

Seattle meanwhile was enduring storm and stress. "The European war" reported the *Post-Intelligencer* of August 23, 1914, "is seriously interfering with New York theatricals." Road shows had slackened almost to a trickle; in dark days, loyal stock companies did their best to spread good cheer. There were many benefits and war plays. Everywhere small acting groups pooled their talents, gaining skill and assurance as they worked. In the East, the Washington Square Players date to war years. In the Northwest, the troubled twenties witnessed the birth of various community acting groups, shortly to replace the resident stock companies as they faded.

Seattle, with its bulging shipyards, received a major body blow during the war years. The influenza epidemic of 1918 temporarily closed its theatres; confusion was added by the general strike of the same year. The "talkies" were invading the scene. Under the combined impact the Wilkes Theatre (stock) closed down in 1922, after six years of yeoman service. Favorite players Phebe Hunt and Norman Hackett bowed out to later stars of a newer, stronger aggregation, the Duffy Players: "the best stock company on the Pacific Coast," who acquired their own theatre, the President. Operating on a larger circuit, their seasoned stars for five years (1925-1930) alternated at branch theatres in Portland, Spokane, San Francisco and Los Angeles. They also used guest stars. But stock itself was on the way out.

In this new-century turmoil, however, the theatre was putting down exploring roots; in the Northwest, geography played a part. Riding the long swell of western migration, southern Oregon received some notable additions. Far back in the '60s, in a snow-choked Minnesota village, a Methodist minister had hauled home by bob-sled a four-octave melodeon for the use of his brood. By its aid, five of his ten children were to become expert musicians. Two of the brothers, Ed and George Andrews, stage-struck after viewing opera in the big city, Minneapolis, tried their own hands at the game—and with striking success. Later setting forth in wagons for a long trek through the "rail fence circuit" of the Midwest and South, they presented *Pinafore, The Doctor of Alcantra, The Chimes of Normandy* and other favorites to receptive crowds. Joined by singing relatives, the Andrews Family became well known as pioneers in good opera for the masses. Several of them achieved high artistic rating.

The wagons were replaced by luxurious private cars, in coast to coast billings; the repertoire, competently staged, had widened. Ed Andrews, cast as Ko-Ko in *The Mikado,* repeated his featured role 1,200 times. Soprano Nellie Andrews was starred by the Boston Lyric Company. At their height, in the '90s, the Andrews Opera Company presented an entire summer season at their own hotel on Lake Minnetonka, served by a branch line of the Northern Pacific Railway.

Touring the country, they had acquired western fever—mainly in the lush Rogue River orchard country. With the new century, under stress of family grief, they decided to emigrate. Brothers Ed, Will and George, joined by some fifty ex-members of the company settled in 1903 near Medford, Oregon, in a unique musical colony which for several decades shaped dramatic tastes thereabouts. Down through the 1920s and later, a brilliant succession of light operas, stage plays and oratorios were presented.

In addition, George Andrews directed the touring Medford Choral Society. The brothers also coached southern Oregon's annual operatic festival, which drew visitors by car or train from long distances. Large casts and choruses were furnished by the community; a skilled technician from the Pathe' Studios, Hollywood, joined their ranks, creating novel revolving sets for an outdoor production of *Robin Hood* at the Midsummer Festival of 1924. Singing the lead in this was James Stevens, husband of Edith Andrews, and a distinguished grand opera star of the period.

Stevens, a man ahead of his time, pioneered in such movements as opera sung in English and the use of native themes. In many tours of the country, he was co-starred with brilliant artists: Rose Cecelia Shay, Bessie Abbott, Schumann-Heink, Jefferson de Angelis, often under contract with New York impresario Henry Savage. Actor as well as singer, he was featured by the St. Louis Festival and the San Francisco Opera Company. He created one of the roles in the Broadway premier of *Everyman,* and was chosen by De Koven for the title role in a revival of *Rob Roy.* Much admired and esteemed in his adopted home, he sang often in Portland, Seattle and elsewhere, after the western migration. As failing health prescribed the warmth of the Rogue River Valley, he there organized a glee club that won distinction on tour.

The Andrews clan numbered other accomplished musicians and artists. Grace Andrews Fiero, protege of Belasco, scored on the stage in *Rose of the Rancho,* as understudy for Frances Starr. A second generation carried on with vigor and charm. Caroline Andrews Werner, daughter of George, was the first featured soprano of NBC, billed as the "Lark;" her husband also a musician. Well down through the thirties, they were key figures in dramatic circles.

Here also, at Ashland, only twelve miles south, the nation's first permanent Elizabethan theatre came to life under the guiding hand of Angus Bowmer, actor and professor of English at the Southern Oregon College of Education. Begun in August of 1935, it still retains the verve of a yearling colt, its audiences growing with each year. Each August, under summer skies, upon a new Tudor stage fashioned after that of the Fortune Theatre, a changing repertory of four Shakespeare plays engrosses spectators.

For its beginnings, a reconditioned Chautauqua Bowl served as buffer for early losses by fire. Nearby Lithia Park with its serene swans has added atmosphere; a Tudor Fair, with period costumes, now lends mirth and color. The month-long session is opened with fanfare, and the presence of assembled dignitaries. The plays are done in swift action, and as lusty as the Bard would have wished. Drawn by skilled direction, actors come from every region. Founder Bowmer, a Shakespeare expert inspired by Stratford, was joined by Dr. Margery Bailey of Stanford for summer background courses. Encouraged by scholarships, here are trained promising young actors. A sustained and highly enthusiastic community interest has warmed the lively enterprise throughout its growth and expansion. Townsmen roundly enjoy the plays, as do the swelling crowds who for a quarter-century have shared the freshness of an ageless source. Just completed is a new and larger theatre, financed by state-wide contribution and farther, and aided also by prominent theatre folk, thus to ensure its promise for the future.

During the twenties, the casual duel between actor and machine quickened. Strange contraptions, dreamed up by the wizard Edison, had appeared; the noisy nickelodeons, gritty phonographs ablare, had edged uptown from cheap skid road store shows. The silent "flickers," unrolling Keystone comedies and Great Train Robberies, had become the more potent "talkies." Highbrow support was given by the German expressionistic films; the first fuzzy news reels made them almost respectable. Speech and mood music, added in 1926 during a presentation of *Don Juan* featuring John Barrymore, increased their spell. Up rose the inimitable W. C. Fields, the vampire Theda Bara, the wistful Mary Pickford. With the wide success of Al Jolson in "The Jazz Singer," the machine made its first serious threat to the legitimate stage.

Early casualties of the talkies were the gypsy tent shows, which had easily survived the silent films. Displaced actors took refuge in vaudeville, in nightclub floor shows, or in the motion pictures themselves. The major vaudeville circuits, the Orpheum and Pantages, expanded swiftly during the thirties, either leasing old theatres or building new ones.

But vaudeville itself was to be crowded by the machine. The "pictures" were cheap; they were easy to transport, and somewhat less prone to disability—and temperament—than the human actor; they gave quick and easy entertainment. But the age-old human urge to act was not so easily disposed of. Nor was the matter of drama itself so simple.

Racked by change and the machine, the twenties witnessed a notable growth. As road shows dwindled and stock faded out, all over the country, in towns little and big, informal acting groups sprang up, aiming to furnish year-round theatre. Self-conscious and often clumsy, they gave an outlet to an innate urge. And there was something about living people right before you. The "meat actors," as the New Englanders called them, you could reach out and feel. What's more, people liked good plays, first-hand.

Nursemaids to these community acting groups were staid Drama Leagues, just then appearing. Amateurish though they undeniably were, these intent study groups, sponsoring playwriting contests, stray road shows—almost anything dramatic—did timely service during a transition. In the Northwest as elsewhere, every town of any size had its eager circle of "Torchbearers," as they were often dubbed. They too were to give way to change. But in fading they left far sturdier offspring: the earthy Little Theatres of the nation, many of which had sprung up within their ranks. Some were to become major dramatic centers, and taking over from the vanishing stock companies the business of providing theatre for the masses, they often developed original techniques.

The masses, of course, meant just plain people everywhere, and the story of these resurgent groups is even now far from finished. On the contrary, stage folk themselves now view the Little Theatres and the more professional university schools of drama as likely roots for such theatre as may yet emerge. They are, at any rate, useful creators of what is known, with increasing respect, as "Theatre, U.S.A." Hard-working groups in the main, they pursue their aim of turning out theatre that may be enjoyed by people around them. Most glamorous figure in the dramatic picture of the nation is still, needless to say, its professional stage centered on and off Broadway, plagued by the problems of our time.

Techniques evolved within such far apart non-professional centers as the Dallas Little Theatre and the University of Washington School of Drama, for example, have become incorporated within modern stage practice. The University of Wisconsin has been active in fostering experiments with grass roots theatre; so too have North Dakota's Black Hill Players. California's Pasadena Playhouse has sent forth many young actors to Broadway, as have a dozen others now well established in East or West. The South's Barter Theatre has evolved unique methods for survival; New Orleans' Vieux Carre' has its own distinctive tradition. Add the robust crew of summer stock or "barn" theatres. All of them, like the ancient wrestler, Anteus, somehow draw hidden strength as they touch earth.

It would be impossible here to relate the tale of the Northwest's numerous community groups. Most towns of size have some such active group, their efforts in furnishing year-round theatre ranging from the awkward to challenging experiment by skilled professionals. All of them are avid patrons of current Broadway releases, together with stray classics and tested oldtimers. Not all of them own their own theatres, but for Oregon, an account of two groups who have built their own playhouses may perhaps by typical.

The transition from stock to community theatre is readily apparent in the acting groups of Portland. Its first Little Theatre—the Red Lantern Players—was formed in 1920 by George Natanson, lately leading man in a season of sparkling musicals presented by the Baker Stock Company. Liking the West, he returned to direct a series of favorite plays the following year, most of them sponsored by the local Drama League. A playing group was formed, which even essayed the somber *Hedda Gabler*. During the season of 1922-23 they toured nearby hamlets, reliving the exciting adventures of early troupers as audiences huddled around pot-bellied stoves, while actors froze in chilly dressing rooms. But, young and ardent, the play was as ever the thing. Among them was youthful Earle Larrimore, then employed by the local gas company, but mad about theatre. His later rise to lead roles in New York's Theatre Guild accents the function of the Little Theatres in training future actors.

Shortly thereafter (1922-26) the Portland Labor College Players charged on stage, directed by Doris Smith, dynamic lover of the drama and later pillar of the city's Civic Theatre. Presenting a series of down-to-earth dramas, they added in 1925 plays by local authors. With the addition of new actors, and known as the Portland Playcrafters, they ran until 1929.

A contemporary group, emphasizing the more esoteric aspects of theatre, were the Bess Whitcomb Players, organized in 1926, and named for their director. A series of thoughtful and work-manlike dramas were presented, and after lively feuding, the two groups merged in 1929 to form the present Portland Civic Theatre. This sizable group has built its own theatre, which includes a handsome Blue Room for arena plays. Under paid professional direction, it runs the year round, presenting a succession of plays on both stages, together with summer musicals in an outdoor patio. They support also a thriving Children's Theatre, and sponsor a summer theatre workshop.

At Eugene, a university town next in population, avid players in 1926 formed their robust Very Little Theatre, the name long an amiable misnomer. Outgrowing in turn an empty drugstore and a drafty county fair building, they erected in 1950 their own modern theatre — well equipped and comfortably free from mortgages. Remarkable here is the degree of community goodwill and participation achieved, perhaps because from the first they have been completely self supporting, asking no favor or sub-sidies. A true community group, they present each year five or more well-staged plays, ranging from "corn shows" to such literate offerings as a first production of Theodore Morrison's poetic drama, *The Dream of Alcestis,* with the author out from Harvard for the occasion. They share with the excellent University Theatre in providing drama for a growing town.

Little Theatres have long been active at Salem, the state's capital, evolving from an early and militant Drama League; Medford has its thriving Footlighters, Albany an eager group. There are community theatres at Florence, Coos Bay and Reeds-port on the coast, inland at Oswego, Cottage Grove and smaller towns. Though they do not own their own theatres, they function in suitable town halls or auditoriums, staging plays for public pleasure—or their own.

Washington offers a lengthy list, headed by theatre-conscious Tacoma, earlier stronghold of the Drama League, and with a membership of hundreds. Idaho and Montana repeat the pattern. Many of these groups have season tickets, giving from four to six plays yearly. The massed contribution to the public well-being is both lively and constructive.

Good theatre is often found on stages of the various university and college schools of drama. Usually well equipped, under professional supervision and with somewhat more freedom for experiment than is possible elsewhere, their place in the evolving American theatre is undeniably creative. And this not only from their function of training young actors

The University of Washington, for example, offers good year-round theatre to a cosmopolitan city of 500,000 inhabitants, from three actively producing centers. At its Penthouse Theatre, built in 1940, originated the use of the "arena stage" now so common throughout the entire country. During the late '30s, students of Washington's School of Drama staged in the round plays of Pirandello, Ibsen and contemporary playwrights with striking results. Employment of its stripped, bare patterns for sophisticated modern comedy or classic drama from here spread outward. Its novel Show Boat, moored on the nearby shores of Lake Washington gives congenial setting for more earthy productions and musicals. Both are well patronized by townsmen. Operas and the larger more formal productions are mounted at veteran Meany Hall. Recently acquired is The Playhouse, on the edge of the campus, formerly operated by Mr. and Mrs. Burton James. Its School of the Theatre offers training in every aspect of stage craft. Members of its faculty have also shared in productions of the Aqua Theatre on Lake Washington and in plays given by the Juvenile Theatre, Inc., at a downtown playhouse. Tireless head of all this activity since 1923 is Director Glenn Hughes, himself a playwright and author.

The University of Oregon, enjoying one of the West's most beautiful and modern theatres, has long been the center for both experiment and entrenched tradition. Both the modern and the classics find place in its yearly repertory, imaginatively staged by a staff of professionals. Its ample play areas include as well an Arena Theatre, a smaller experimental tryout theatre for student use, and an outdoor theatre. A companionable Green Room, vast backstage space and advanced stage equipment have made it favorite for Northwest Drama Conferences, gathered to view results of contemporary experiment in lighting or of interpretation of some seldom-staged play by Director Horace Robinson and his staff. For the annual musicals, the School of Music or instructors in modern dance lend a hand. A close connection between town and gown is here evident. Drama is heavily stressed in all neighbor colleges: Oregon State at Corvallis, Reed College in Portland, Portland State, Southern Oregon at Ashland. It flourishes at the University of Portland and Willamette University at Salem.

Montana has favored the regional. Such early directors as Carl Glick, aided by the Montana Masquers' Playwriting Contest, drew in interesting material. Missoula, location of *Frontier* magazine, with a far western slant, long edited by H. G. Merriam, was early site of the Northwest Writers' Conference. Present-day instructors, both at the university and Montana State, include the contemporary in their planned productions.

Neighboring Idaho has also fostered the growth of native roots. Among early productions was the pageant *Idaho,* by Talbot Jennings, later script writer at Hollywood for *Mutiny on the Bounty* and other films. Today's directors here as elsewhere choose their repertories with catholic taste. In return, a wholesome acquaintance with drama, old and new, is bred both in audience and students—a conditioning to the subject matter of the theatre which has its own slow force.

Road shows, meanwhile, still make the rounds, mainly Broadway hits featuring big names, drawing a quota of devoted fans ... Change has brought responsive change, the better to mirror the times they so faithfully reflect.

As for the theatre itself—shunning the mantle of the seer—it seems likely by now that the demise of that fabulous invalid is far from imminent, bringing at least a nagging question: What, in the slick age of the machine, finally happens to its makers? One recalls that the human urge to act is ageless; that despite admittedly fascinating gadgets, the actual presence of living actors within reach gives an audience reaction more intimate, more direct than admittedly glamorous shadows on a screen . . . Summer stock persists in every state, in assorted friendly barns, lusty as ever; there is even Shakespeare in Radio City, tented musicals here or there. The urban schools of acting go on turning out young actors. And even in the Big City, with its cut-throat business pressures, one may—with good luck—get a ticket to *My Fair Lady* years from now, at far too high prices.

Can it be that the scapegrace theatre, so notoriously fond of new scenes, may have some unexpected curtains ahead?

Selected / # BIBLIOGRAPHY

Prime sources of this book have been first-hand interviews with people connected with early theatres of the Oregon Country. These have underwritten off-stage memories of settlers who enjoyed plays and players in a passing frontier. Acknowledgments of this sterling aid may be found elsewhere.

Direct accounts of stage events as recorded in newspapers or periodicals of the day have been as potent in re-creating a vanished day. From a long list in the Oregon Historical Society library and elsewhere some of the most often consulted follow:

PERIODICALS

Bonvill's Western Monthly (Portland).
The Golden Era (San Francisco), 1891 on.
Inn-Side News (ed. by Phil Metschan), 1943-46.
Music and Drama (San Francisco), 1884-85.
The Native Son (Salem).
Oregon Historical Quarterly (Portland).
Oregon Magazine (Salem), 1918 on.
The Rose City Magazine (Portland), 1908-1909.
The Spectator (Portland).
Theatre Arts (New York).
The West Shore (Portland), 1875-91.

NEWSPAPERS

Astorian (Weekly; Daily; Morning), 1873-1926.
Blue Mountain American (Sumpter).
Blue Mountain Eagle (Canyon City).
Bumblebee (Coos County), 1884.
Capital City Chronicle (Salem), 1867.
Chronicle (Vancouver), 1860.
Coast Mail (Marshfield).
Colonist (Victoria, B. C.), 1886.
Columbian (Vancouver).
Courier-Herald (Oregon City).
Daily Record (Salem), 1867.
Democratic Times (Jacksonville), 1880-84.
East Oregonian (Pendleton).
Enterprise (Oregon City).
Eugene City Review, 1863.
Gazette (Corvallis), 1889 on.
Grant County Journal (Prairie City), 1917-26.
Independent (Vancouver), 1870-90.
Journal (Albany), 1864-65.

Journal (La Grande).
Mountaineer (The Dalles), 1869.
Oregon Argus (Oregon City), 1855-59.
Oregon Journal (Portland).
Oregon Sentinel (Jacksonville), 1862.
Oregon Spectator (Oregon City), 1845-46.
Oregon State Journal (Eugene).
Oregon Statesman (Salem), 1869 on.
Oregon Weekly Union (Corvallis), 1862.
Oregonian (Portland), 1850 on.
Pioneer and Democrat (Olympia), 1854.
Post-Intelligencer (Seattle).
Record-Courier (Baker).
Register (Vancouver), 1865.
Review (Roseburg), 1900.
Southern Oregon Gazette (Jacksonville), 1861.
Tidings (Ashland), 1909 on.
Times (Seattle).
Times-Mountaineer (The Dalles), 1880.

Assorted diaries, literary and W.P.A. records, scrapbooks, regional manuscripts, house publications of various theatres, playbills and similar sources were also used. The Crandall clipping collection, The Dalles, and the Sayre-Karkeek Theatre Collection, Seattle Public Library, were very useful.

BOOKS

Adams, W. L. *A Melodrama Entitled Treason, Stratagems and Spoils,* by Breakspear ("Oregonian" Office, Portland, 1852).

Bancroft, H. H. *Works* (A. L. Bancroft & Co., San Francisco, 1882-90).

Blankenship, George E. *Lights and Shades of Pioneer Life on Puget Sound,* by a Native Son (Olympia, Washington, 1923).

Blum, Daniel. *A Pictorial History of the American Stage* (Grosset & Dunlap, New York, 1955).

Carson, Wm. G. D. *Letters of Mr. and Mrs. Kean as Regarding Their American Tour* (University of Washington, Seattle, 1945).

Case, Robert O. and Victoria. *We Called It Culture, the Story of Chautauqua* (Doubleday, Garden City, N. Y., 1948).

Clark, D. E. *The West in American History* (Crowell, New York, ca. 1937).

Dodge, Orvil. *Pioneer History of Coos and Curry Counties, Oregon* (Capital Printing Co., Salem, 1898).

Elliott, E. C. *A History of Variety-Vaudeville in Seattle From the Beginning to 1914* (University of Washington, Seattle, 1944).

Fargo, L. F. *The Spokane Story* (Columbia University Press, New York, 1950).

Ferguson, Francis. *The Idea of a Theater* (University of Princeton Press, Princeton, New Jersey, 1949).

Freedley, George and Clark, Barrett H. *History of Modern Drama* (Appleton-Century, New York, 1947).

Gagey, Edmond M. *The San Francisco Stage* (Columbia University Press, New York, 1950).

Grant, Howard F. *The Story of Seattle's Early Theatres* (University of Washington, Seattle, 1934).

Hamid, George E. *Circus* (Sterling Publishing Co., New York, 1950).

Hayes, Jeff W. *Looking Backward at Portland* (Kilham Stationery & Printing Co., Portland, 1911).

History of Baker, Grant, Malheur & Harney Counties (Western Historical Publishing Co., Spokane, 1902).

Holbrook, Stewart H. *The Columbia*, Rivers of America Series (Rinehart, New York, 1956).

Holbrook, Stewart H. *Yankee Exodus* (Macmillan, New York, 1950).

Hussey, J. Adam. *Preliminary Survey of the Historical and Physical Structure of Fort Vancouver* (National Park Service, Region Four, 1949).

Irving, Washington. *Astoria* (Putnam, New York, 1897).

McMinn, George R. *The Theatre of the Golden Era in California* (Caxton, Caldwell, Idaho, 1941).

MacNeal, Violet. *Four White Horses and a Brass Band* (Garden City Press, New York, 1947).

Massett, Stephen. *Drifting About or What Jeems Pipes of Pipeville Saw-and-Did* (Carleton, New York, 1863).

Matthews, Brander. *The Development of the Drama* (Scribners, New York, 1903).

Meade, Edwards. *Doubling Back, the Autobiography of an Actor* (Hammond Press, Chicago, 1916).

Miller, Joaquin. Plays *(The Danites; Forty-Nine; Tally Ho!; An Oregon Idyll)*.

Morris, Carl. *Curtain Time, The Story of the American Theatre* (Random House, New York, 1952).

Oregon, End of the Trail, American Guide Series (Binfords & Mort, Portland, 1940).

Parrington, Vernon L. *Main Currents in American Thought* (Harcourt, Brace & Co., New York, 1927).

Pioneer Women's Club. *Reminiscences of Oregon Pioneers* (East Oregonian Publishing Co., Pendleton, 1937).

Powell, Lyman. *Historic Towns of the Western States* (Putnam, New York, 1901).

Pyper, George. *The Romance of an Old Playhouse* (Seagull Press, Salt Lake City, 1928).

Quinn, A. H. *A History of the American Drama From the Beginning to the Civil War* (Crofts & Company, New York, 1936).

Rich, E. E. (ed.) *McLoughlin's Fort Vancouver Letters,* Third Series, 1844-46 (Hudson's Bay Record Society, London, 1944).

Rourke, Constance. *Troupers of the Gold Coast or The Rise of Lotta Crabtree* (Harcourt, Brace & Co., New York, 1928).

Ruggles, Eleanor. *Prince of Players,* Edwin Booth (Norton, New York, 1933).

Sengstacken, Agnes. *Destination, West!* (Binfords & Mort, Portland, 1942).

Skinner, Constance Lindsay. *Adventurers of Oregon,* Chronicles of America Series (Yale University Press, New Haven, 1920).

Skinner, Cornelia Otis. *Family Circle* (Houghton-Mifflin, Boston, 1948).

Skinner, Otis. *Footlights and Spotlights* (Bobbs-Merrill, Indianapolis, 1924).

Theatrical and Circus Life (Sun Publishing Co., St. Louis, 1882).

Victor, Frances Fuller. *All Over Oregon and Washington* (John H. Carmany & Co., San Francisco, 1872).

Walling, A. G. *History of Southern Oregon* (Walling, Portland, 1884).

Walling, A. G. *Illustrated History of Lane County* (Walling, Portland, 1884).

Warde, Frederic. *Fifty Years of Make Believe* (Times-Mirror Press, Los Angeles, 1923).

Washington, the Evergreen State, American Guide Series (Binfords & Mort, Portland, 1941).

Whiffin, Mrs. Thomas. *Keeping Off the Shelf* (Dutton, New York, 1928).

Winter, William. *Life of David Belasco* (2 volumes, Moffat, Yard & Company, New York, 1918).

INDEX